Implementing Student-Athlete Programming

In *Implementing Student-Athlete Programming*, scholar-practitioners provide an approachable and comprehensive overview of how to design, implement, and sustain best practices in the growing area of student-athlete affairs. Exploring research approaches and critical frames for thinking about student-athlete programming while covering topics such as the current context, challenges, programmatic approaches to support, and trends for the future, this resource also highlights programs that are effective in supporting students to success. This book provides higher education practitioners with the tools they need to effectively work with student-athletes to not only transition to college, but to develop meaningful personal, social, career, and leadership development experiences as they prepare for the transition to life after sport.

Kristina M. Navarro is Assistant Professor of Professional Practice in the Graduate School of Education and Senior Associate Athletic Director for Leadership Development and Strategic Partnerships at Rutgers University, USA.

Lisa Melanie Rubin is Assistant Professor of Student Services in Intercollegiate Athletics at Kansas State University, USA.

Geoff Mamerow is Assistant Director of Learning Outcomes Assessment in the Office of Planning and Assessment at The Pennsylvania State University, USA.

Implementing Student-Athlete Programming

A Guide for Supporting College Athletes

Kristina M. Navarro,
Lisa Melanie Rubin,
and Geoff Mamerow

First published 2020
by Routledge
52 Vanderbilt Avenue, New York, NY 10017

and by Routledge
2 Park Square, Milton Park, Abingdon, Oxon, OX14 4RN

Routledge is an imprint of the Taylor & Francis Group, an informa business

© 2020 Taylor & Francis

The right of Kristina M. Navarro, Lisa Melanie Rubin, and Geoff Mamerow to be identified as authors of this work has been asserted by them in accordance with sections 77 and 78 of the Copyright, Designs and Patents Act 1988.

All rights reserved. No part of this book may be reprinted or reproduced or utilised in any form or by any electronic, mechanical, or other means, now known or hereafter invented, including photocopying and recording, or in any information storage or retrieval system, without permission in writing from the publishers.

Trademark notice: Product or corporate names may be trademarks or registered trademarks, and are used only for identification and explanation without intent to infringe.

Library of Congress Cataloging-in-Publication Data
Names: Navarro, Kristina M., author. | Rubin, Lisa Melanie, author. | Mamerow, Geoffrey, author.
Title: Implementing student athlete programming : a guide for supporting college athletes / By Kristina M. Navarro, Lisa Melanie Rubin, and Geoffrey Mamerow.
Description: New York : Routledge, 2019. | Includes bibliographical references.
Identifiers: LCCN 2019015439 | ISBN 9781138732421 (hardback) | ISBN 9781138732438 (paperback) | ISBN 9781315188454 (ebook)
Subjects: LCSH: College athletes–Education–United States. | School-to-work transition–United States. | School improvement programs–United States.
Classification: LCC LC2580.6 .N32 2019 | DDC 796.04/3–dc23
LC record available at https://lccn.loc.gov/2019015439

ISBN: 978-1-138-73242-1 (hbk)
ISBN: 978-1-138-73243-8 (pbk)
ISBN: 978-1-315-18845-4 (ebk)

Typeset in Sabon
by Newgen Publishing UK

 Printed in the United Kingdom by Henry Ling Limited

To my mentors and colleagues of N4A who have pioneered the path for this developing field and former student-athletes who continue to inspire, lift and rise.

– KMN

To my Dad, Harold Herbert Levine, who encouraged me to write and read all of it.

– LMR

Contents

Preface ix

1 Introduction, Context, and Chapter Overviews 1

2 Contemporary Context of Athletics in Higher Education 12

3 The Student-Athlete Experience: Opportunities and Challenges 28

4 Programs That Support Student-Athletes 52

5 Program Models Across Divisions: Case Studies at Division I, II, and III Institutions 78

6 Assessment and Data-Driven Practices in Intercollegiate Athletics 111

7 Cross-Program Collaboration and Strategic Partnerships: Evolving Models of Strategic Partnership and Inter-Program Collaboration in Athletics 131

8 The Future of Student-Athlete Development 160

Index 174

Preface

The programs, practices, and policies designed to support student-athletes are becoming increasingly important as the commercialization of college sport and time demands of student-athletes take center stage across the United States. The placement of intercollegiate athletic departments within institutions of higher education continues to require a balance of academics and athletics for student-athletes to remain eligible and compete at the intercollegiate level. However, the practice of developing student-athletes beyond the Xs and 0s, Academic Progress Rate (APR) and Graduation Success Rate (GSR) scores has drastically evolved over the last ten years. Consequently, the important role student-athlete development professionals play has come to the forefront and requires enhanced attention to develop 21st-century professionals who support this distinctive population. These individuals are charged with supporting student-athletes not only as they transition to college, but also to help them develop meaningful personal, social, career, and leadership development experiences during college as they prepare for life after sport.

To this end, the authors of this book represent a cross section of scholar-practitioners who have actively worked and studied to develop best practices for student development programs in higher education and prepare the next generation of practitioners who will understand, implement, assess, and evolve programming for student-athletes. The collective experiences of the authors provide a diverse range of experiences which inform the core of this text. Dr. Kristina Navarro, current Senior Associate Athletic Director for Leadership Development and Strategic Partnerships at Rutgers University, has spent 12 years focused on identifying best practices in student-athlete holistic development programs as a tenured faculty member at the Division III level and senior-level executive in the front office of the National Collegiate Athletics Association (NCAA) Division I Power 5 conference. Dr. Lisa Rubin, a faculty member focusing on the study of student services in intercollegiate athletics, aims to empower the future of scholar-practitioners in the field by providing research knowledge and opportunities to those in the field of student-athlete services. She began her career in athletic academic advising and student-athlete development and served as a practitioner before her pursuit of contributing research to the field. Dr. Geoff Mamerow has studied and worked broadly in higher education. His research has focused on program evaluation and administration, in particular with respect to the types of programs and experiences institutions design and administer to support students who are new to college or who are transitioning to the world of post-secondary education. He has worked on institutional effectiveness and he has held leadership roles at multiple institutions in assessment and institutional research offices. The authors are highly involved in various organizations, including the American Education Research Association (AERA) Research Focus on Education and Sport Special Interest Group, Association for the Study of Higher Education (ASHE), National Association of Student Affairs Professionals (NASPA), NACADA: The Global Community for Academic Advising, and the N4A: National Association of Academic and Student-Athlete Development Professionals (N4A). The evolution of student-athlete development has taken shape in the last ten years across these scholarship and practitioner organizations, and the work of their members has informed the topics and details found in this book.

The genesis of this textbook can be traced back some three years to a series of conversations we held at an N4A annual convention. Work that began between the trio on methods to best assess program pilots for NCAA student-athlete development programs evolved as the field continued to evolve. This work is the collective overview of many hours spent on conference calls, advisory boards, and leadership committees to understand and define the field of student-athlete development with our colleagues across NCAA divisions I, II, and III. We are excited to present to you what we have found since then, including background on student-athletes, the programs that support them, the institutions in which they exist, and the data-driven practices and recommendations that we as scholar-practitioners who work at the nexus of intercollegiate athletics and higher education believe to be essential to the aspiring, new, or even seasoned student-athlete development professional.

Chapter One

Introduction, Context, and Chapter Overviews

The purpose of this book is to provide an overview and exploration of programs and practices common to the world of contemporary student-athlete affairs. This burgeoning field continues to evolve and change at all levels of intercollegiate athletics. Initially, athletic departments' focus was on academic support for student-athletes as the need arose. College sport governing bodies increased academic regulations for athletic participation, and as the rules became more complex, supporting athletes in their navigation of the academic rigor in college while balancing their role as athletes required intentional resources for this student population.

However, given the extraordinary challenges that student-athletes face while balancing the dual roles of student and athlete in college, student-athlete development (also known as "life skills") became an important addition, whether in programming or through hiring additional staff in student-athlete support services units. As campuses have added facilities specifically to serve student-athletes in these endeavors, an expansion of resources, staff, and programming has become prevalent in the field, especially among institutions that have sizeable athletic budgets. Athletic departments already utilize their facilities, resources, and staff in recruiting student-athletes to their institutions, so more support for student development and academics is certainly a selling point, especially to their parents.

This is an exciting time for student-athlete services professionals and those seeking to enter the field. As more need arises, departments will expand and look for talents in a variety of student development areas, including leadership development, career development, personal enhancement, mental health and well-being, diversity and inclusion, and learning strategies, among others. The hub of professional development for this field is the N4A. Initially, the National Collegiate Athletic Association (NCAA) hosted its own professional development for the life skills/student-athlete development area for its member institutions, and other governing bodies mentioned in Chapter 2 have their own approaches. In 2015, the NCAA transitioned that charge to N4A, and that has led to specific tracks at its national conference and a Professional Development Institute (PDI) on student-athlete development, with trained faculty, who are practitioners and experts in the field (Leach, 2015). Its curriculum and core competencies are discussed further in Chapter 8.

There is often a disconnect between student affairs professionals on campus and student-athlete services professionals, regardless of where they are housed. Many student-athlete support staff feel misunderstood by other parts of campus, and even by athletic administrators as to what their role is or what their responsibilities are to students and the athletic department (Rubin & Moreno-Pardo, 2018). It is critical, as this field continues to grow, that cross-campus collaboration take place to engage professionals from campus with student-athlete support staff, to prevent burnout. Intercollegiate athletics in itself is a stressful place to work with intense pressures, and burnout can affect talented professionals that institutions hope to retain (Rubin & Moreno-Pardo, 2018). Examples of collaboration are presented in Chapter 5, which shares models at three NCAA institutions in divisions I, II, and III.

There are so many approaches to offering student-athlete support on college campuses, whether housed in athletics or in academic affairs/ under the provost's office, or in another administrative area. There is no one model practice, and resources are not uniform across campuses, even within the same athletic conference or across peer institutions. Some units have one person on staff to support hundreds of student-athletes, and others have 20 to support a similar number. There is definitely no one-size-fits-all design of student-athlete services in any category of athletic program or institution type. What is key for growth and success aside from campus collaboration is the connection between professionals who work in this field through networking, involvement in N4A (the premier professional organization), and targeted professional development.

To fulfill our purpose, this book includes: (a) explanation of the current context of athletics within higher education, including NCAA governance structures and the role athletic departments play in mediating student-athletes' experiences in college; (b) discussion of the challenges educational and developmental challenges student-athletes face within and as a result of that context; (c) in-depth description and illustration of the many varied programmatic approaches institutions and their athletic departments take to effectively support their student-athletes; (d) presentation of several illustrative cases studies exploring student-athlete programming in practice, including a model Division I comprehensive athletics program at the University of Nebraska, a model Division II athletics program focused on campus collaboration at West Chester University, and a model Division III athletics program focused on the high-impact Leadership Academy program at the University of Wisconsin-Whitewater (UW-Whitewater); (e) description of, and a guide to assessing the effectiveness of student-athlete support programs; (f) presentation of an additional case study focused on strategic partnerships developed by Rutgers University's athletic department; and (g) identification and discussion of trends and implications to monitor for the future of supporting student-athletes through programming in higher education.

The genesis of this book is rooted in our experiences studying and developing programs to support student success in general and the unique population of student-athletes in particular. As scholars and practitioners, we are always searching for new ideas, research, and inspiration for what we do to support the students we work with as professionals. In our search for new materials and innovative practices to support our work, it became clear how few resources exist to guide the growing number of professionals working in student-athlete support. While student affairs units have proliferated recently, the specific group of practitioners focusing on student-athletes has grown over the last few decades, because student-athletes as a population on college campuses have increasingly been identified as having common sets of characteristics, factors, or experiences that put them at risk for several negative outcomes in higher education. These professionals are the most diverse staff within athletic departments, and bring a richness of talent, experience, and perspectives to the development of innovative programs that support student-athletes and their college experience (NCAA, 2019).

In response to the growing need, institutions have sought to develop programs that address distinctive challenges faced by student-athletes, and there has been great diversity in their approaches, as well as the effectiveness and impact of those approaches for students, athletic departments, and institutions as a whole. Our aim in this book is to shed light on a range of topics by explaining the student-athlete context, discussing factors that affect that context, and then both describing and comparing programs that support them.

Along the way, we will analyze these programs to reveal practices that are both theoretically sound, but also tested in practice. In so doing, we hope to offer ideas about how to successfully design, implement, and sustain similar programs with an emphasis on high impact. To further unpack these concepts, this book will take an in-depth look at how athletic departments can assess the effectiveness of these programs and best support contemporary student-athletes for life after intercollegiate sport. We endeavor that each chapter can provide a point of departure

INTRODUCTION, CONTEXT, AND CHAPTER OVERVIEWS

for the aspiring practitioner within the world of student-athlete support programming. Each chapter starts with a broad view, then narrows in focus to explore and discuss issues that are critical to the practice of student affairs in athletic departments and other units that support student-athletes.

Chapter 2, *Contemporary Context of Athletics in Higher Education*, provides the reader with a high-level overview of governance in intercollegiate athletics. It reviews the role of sport governing bodies such as the NCAA, athletic governance structures, the contemporary divisions and conference organizations, and provides explanations of how those governing bodies and structures co-exist with institutions of higher education. Where appropriate, it recounts the history and development of these relationships to provide the context necessary to extrapolate trends in what is a constantly developing field. The chapter also discusses the increasing involvement of student-athletes in the governance of the structures and organization in which they operate, as well as their growing influence and power in decision-making that impacts their education and competition. Finally, it covers recent developments in conference realignment, the impact that the development of student-athlete support programming and athletic departments have had on colleges and universities, as well as the role(s) athletic departments play in mediating the complex rules and relationships between governance bodies, institutions, and their student-athletes.

The purpose of Chapter 3, *The Student-Athlete Experience: Opportunities and Challenges*, is to provide an in-depth review of the scholarly literature documenting the student-athlete experience in college. This chapter reviews single and multi-institution studies exploring the many challenges student-athletes face, in particular those related to time demands and pressure to perform. In addition to painting a picture of the common and distinctive characteristics of the student-athlete experience, it discusses and dispels myths about student-athletes as well. Drawing on both historical and contemporary research, the chapter describes internal and external barriers to personal and career development student-athletes often experience, as well as institutional practices that impact many student-athletes today, such as academic and social isolation, and other academic policies and practices including clustering. It considers the changing generation of student-athletes from Millennials and their challenges to those of Generation Z. The chapter concludes by introducing and discussing several relevant theoretical frameworks derived from research into the student-athlete experiences that are of particular salience as they are frequently drawn upon, not only to guide current research on student-athletes, but to inform the development of programming meant to address or mediate the risk factors student-athletes experience.

INTRODUCTION, CONTEXT, AND CHAPTER OVERVIEWS

Chapter 4, *Programs That Support Student-Athletes*, introduces and provides in-depth discussion of institutional approaches to developing and administering academic support programming designed to support student-athletes' needs, as well as the fast-growing student-athlete development focus in athletics. It discusses several specific, illustrative program models, including discussion of their roots in the scholarship on student-athletes and their roots in models of student-athlete cognitive and psychosocial development. The chapter includes examples from a range of different institutions, including mission-driven institutions such as Historically Black Colleges and Universities (HBCUs) and further compares and contrasts common types of programs offered across divisions. The chapter concludes with consideration of the physical spaces and constructed environments that have come to define the "sense of place" in which student-athletes spend their time living and working out their roles as students and athletes.

Chapter 5, *Program Models in Divisions: Case Studies at Division I, II, and III Institutions*, presents three case studies wrought as comprehensive descriptions of how a Division I, II, and III institution each deliver student-athlete support programming on their campuses. The first model features the program and approach at the University of Nebraska-Lincoln, and includes in-depth discussion of the history and origin of Nebraska's approach to holistic programming, including how it is currently administered, its signature practices, budgetary and staffing considerations, and outcomes.

The chapter also provides a Division II case study focusing on West Chester University (WCU) and its approach to delivering high-quality, high-value programming. In particular, the case study focuses on WCU's collaborative approach to supporting academic excellence, an approach that leverages a range of campus programs in service to providing academic support for student-athletes.

Finally, the chapter outlines a comprehensive athletic programming approach from the Division III level, by describing the Warhawk Leadership Academy at UW-Whitewater. The program demonstrates a powerful approach to cultivating leadership skills in student-athletes, while also illustrating how practitioners can tether programming to the literature and scholarship on student-athlete development. The program exemplifies data-driven practices to best help students develop leadership skills and succeed in college. The chapter also includes introductory information on program evaluation, as well as guidelines for beginning to develop similar programming at other institutions.

Chapter 6, *Assessment and Data-Driven Practices in Intercollegiate Athletics*, provides a basic primer for the practice of assessment of programming in intercollegiate athletics. It begins by orienting the reader to assessment, its purpose, rationales, and potential then briefly explores examples of assessment reports published in the literature. The bulk of the chapter explores the individual steps in an assessment plan as applied to a fictitious leadership development program designed to support student-athletes. The chapter is designed to serve as a guide and resource for practitioners attempting to design assessment plans for their own programming, in their own contexts, and with their own distinctive student-athlete populations.

Chapter 7, *Cross-Program Collaboration and Strategic Partnerships: Evolving Models of Strategic Partnership and Inter-Program Collaboration in Athletics*, focuses on the case of Rutgers University to explore an approach to delivering student-athlete support programming through strategic partnerships, including the important role that fundraising and development play in intercollegiate athletics. The chapter opens with rich descriptions of the Rutgers programs' organizing pillars, including in-depth discussion of how those foundational organizational principles are derived from the literature and research about what best supports student-athletes. After describing the comprehensive approach to programming, the chapter pivots to reveal how the university delivers the program components through strategic partnership across campus, in the community, and across the nation and even world.

In contrast to other chapters touching on collaborations across programs, this chapter focus on the strategic component, and the importance of positioning for growth and sustainability. Finally, the chapter closes by discussing the important role that development and fundraising increasingly plays in the pursuit of funding to support programming in ways that do not draw from general institutional funds. The discussion includes a basic guide and inventory of steps to consider in forwarding a fundraising or development drive/campaign in the context of intercollegiate athletics.

Finally, Chapter 8, *The Future of Student-Athlete Development*, provides a discussion of lessons learned from the study and administration of student-athlete support programs, presents recommendations for administrators, and shares implications for research, policy, and practice. Drawing upon the book's content and discussion, it plants a flag into the ground about the current state of practice in intercollegiate athletics support programming, but looks to the future by considering limitations of past and contemporary practices, as well as highlighting the promise and potential of future approaches.

TERMS AND DEFINITIONS

In the following sections we present some terms and concepts of note for the reader to keep in mind. This short list includes common topics, ideas, and concepts that arise again and again throughout the book. They are defined below.

INTRODUCTION, CONTEXT, AND CHAPTER OVERVIEWS

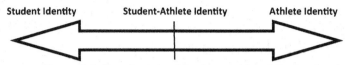

Figure 1.1 Continuum of Student-Athlete Identity

Academic–Athletic Role Conflict: Brewer, Van Raalte, and Linder (1993) defined this type of conflict as the extent to which an individual identifies with athletic and academic roles. Adler and Adler (1987) posit that student-athletes identify with two conflicting roles of association: athletic identity and academic identity. The degree to which one associates with either role can be represented on a continuum (see Figure 1.1).

Individuals who identify with the role of student are situated at the opposite end of the spectrum from those who identify with the role of athlete. Situated in the middle of this spectrum is the student-athlete ideal who identifies equally with both roles. Individuals who identify equally with both roles are considered to not experience role conflict. As individuals encounter different life experiences, their place on this continuum can fluctuate (Brewer et al., 1993)

Assessment: The systematic collection, analysis, and use of information for the purpose of continually improving an educational program or learning experience.

Career Construction: Savickas (2002) defined the term "career construction" as a dynamic process, in which individuals construct their careers by using life themes and experiences to guide choices. The theory of career construction presents a modern approach to Super's (1957) seminal theory of vocational development. This theory has developed in the 21st century to describe the dynamic and evolutionary process of the construct of career development (Savickas, 2002, 2005). We contextualize career construction as the individual process of exploring career opportunities, making informed career decisions, and designing potential career trajectories based on life experiences. Moreover, within the context of this book we define career construction as a process by which students explore, choose, and prepare for career fields informed by life experiences.

Career Identity: The Theory of Career Construction suggests the processes of career construction and identity development are intertwined (Savickas, 2002, 2005). Savickas (2002) posited that in the 21st century individuals continuously describe who they are in terms of their career. Therefore, in the context of this book we refer to career identity as one's chosen career path.

Curriculum Map: A matrix or table that demonstrates the intersection between a program's learning objectives, and the courses, activities, or experiences offered by the program.

Football Bowl Subdivision (FBS): Formerly known as NCAA Division IA, this group of institutions constitutes major NCAA Division I institutions in athletic conferences that offer football programs that play in a combination of playoff and bowl games at the end of a regular season. These institutions tend to have the most resources and funding for their athletic departments and programs. The Power 5 "autonomy" conferences are included in this group.

Football Championship Subdivision (FCS): Formerly known as NCAA Division IAA, this group of institutions constitutes NCAA Division I institutions in athletic conferences that offer football programs that play in a playoff system at the end of the regular season. These institutions tend to have smaller budgets than their FBS counterparts, and play in conferences that are more geographically based or historically based (e.g., made up of HBCUs).

HBCUs: According to Cooper, Cavil, and Cheeks (2014), "HBCUs were established to provide Black Americans with educational opportunities to acquire and to develop skills for survival and upward mobility" (p. 307). The first HBCU, Cheyney University, was established in 1837. Allen and Jewell (2002) explained, "HBCUs have functioned as multifaceted institutions, providing not only education, but also social, political, and religious leadership for the African American community" (p. 242). There are just over 100 in the United States and Virgin Islands in the 2010s (Cooper et al., 2014). At the same time the organization that would become the NCAA formed in 1906, the first Black athletic conference was also formed (Cooper et al., 2014; Smith, 2011).

Identity Foreclosure: Marcia (1966) described identity foreclosure as a premature commitment to an occupation without engaging in exploratory behavior. In relationship to student-athletes, this term is defined as the unwillingness to explore alternatives outside of careers in professional sport (Chartrand & Lent, 1987; Petitpas & Champagne, 1988). Participation in intercollegiate athletics may hinder student-athletes' exploration of careers outside of sport, and in turn, promote identity foreclosure or an affinity to prepare only for careers related to sport (Baillie & Danish, 1992; Petitpas & Champagne, 1988).

Learning Objective: A brief statement of the knowledge, skills, habits or mind, or other qualities that are the goal of participation in a learning activity. This term is often used interchangeably with "learning outcome."

INTRODUCTION, CONTEXT, AND CHAPTER OVERVIEWS

Life After (Intercollegiate) Sport: This term is commonly referred to in literature focusing on the student-athlete experience. It refers to a period of time triggered by two events in a student-athlete's development: (a) exhaustion of eligibility for competition within intercollegiate athletics programs or (b) graduation from an institution of higher education (Jolly, 2008). These two life events may occur at different times, or simultaneously, depending on individual circumstance. In the context of this book, we refer to life after sport as a period of time when an individual satisfies both scenarios of exhausting eligibility and graduating.

Power 5: The Power 5 is a group of NCAA athletic conferences representing 65 institutions. These conferences include the Atlantic Coast Conference (ACC), Big 12 Conference, Big Ten Conference, Pacific-12 Conference (PAC-12), and Southeastern Conference (SEC). These institutions have the authority to put forth legislation that affects only students in these conferences and vote. These institutions offer athletic programs that have the highest budgets and expenditures in college sports. They are also known as the Division I autonomy or autonomous conferences.

Letterwinner: This term refers to a student-athlete who has participated on an athletic team representing the university for a full season in the sport and an academic year. Athletic departments offer letterwinner clubs that are essentially alumni organizations including former letterwinners from their institution.

Student-Athlete Development: This term refers to a burgeoning field that encompasses the holistic development of student-athletes, previously known as life skills. The NCAA initially offered what was called Challenging Athletes' Minds for Personal Success (CHAMPS)/Life Skills as an initiative for student-athlete development, launching in 1994 (NCAA, 1999). Relating to the idea that college is a time when students are developing their identity, student-athlete development approaches support student-athletes at this time of transition and growth through specialized staff and programming, and these specialisms are typically housed within athletic departments. Student-athlete development may or may not be part of the academic support provided to student-athletes, as sometimes institutions will have both together in the same unit. At many institutions, student-athlete services professionals provide both academic support and student-athlete development programs. At others, student-athlete development professionals are specialists who work in the Academic Support unit or in their own units. In 2015, the NCAA partnered with the N4A to transition professional development for this field to N4A (Leach, 2015).

Training Table: The training table refers to a dining hall or meal plan available specifically for student-athletes. This benefit for student-athletes is often organized in tandem with a nutritionist or at least with the nutritional needs of active athletes in mind. Meals can be offered for breakfast, lunch, and dinner as well as for traveling teams on the road.

REFERENCES

Adler, P., & Adler, P. A. (1987). Role conflict and identity salience: College athletics and the academic role. *Social Science Journal, 24*(2), 443–450.

Allen, W. R., & Jewell, J. O. (2002). A backward glance forward: Past, present, and future perspectives on historically Black colleges and universities. *Review of Higher Education, 25*(3), 241–261.

Baillie, P. H., & Danish, S. J. (1992). Understanding the career transition of athletes. *The Sport Psychologist, 6*(1), 77–98.

Brewer, B. W., Van Raalte, J. L., & Linder, D. E. (1993). Athletic identity: Hercules' muscle or Achilles heel? *International Journal of Sport Psychology, 24*, 237–254.

Chartrand, J. M., & Lent, R. W. (1987). Sports counseling: Enhancing the development of the student-athlete. *Journal of Counseling and Development, 66*(4), 164–167.

Cooper, J. N., Cavil, J. K., & Cheeks, G. (2014). The state of intercollegiate athletics at HBCUs: Past, present, and persistence. *Journal of Issues in Intercollegiate Athletics, 7*, 307–332.

Jolly, J. C. (2008). Raising the question #9: Is the student-athlete population unique? And why should we care? *Communication Education, 57*(1), 145–151.

Leach, K. C. (2015, October 16). *NCAA, N4A to partner on life skills professional development.* Retrieved from www.ncaa.org/about/resources/media-center/news/ncaa-n4a-partner-life-skills-professional-development

Marcia, J. E. (1966). Development and validation of ego-identity status. *Journal of Personality and Social Psychology, 3*(5), 551.

National Collegiate Athletic Association (NCAA). (1999). *NCAA CHAMPS/Life Skills Program* [Brochure]. Indianapolis, IN.

NCAA. (2019). *Race and gender demographics database.* Retrieved from www.ncaa.org/about/resources/research/diversity-research

Petitpas, A. L., & Champagne, D. E. (1988). Developmental programming for intercollegiate athletes. *Journal of College Student Development, 29*, 454–460.

Rubin, L. M., & Moreno-Pardo, M. D. (2018). Burnout among student-athlete services professionals. *Journal of Higher Education Athletics and Innovation*, *1*(3), 1–25.

Savickas, M. L. (2002). Career construction: A developmental theory of vocational behavior. In D. Brown & Associates (Eds.), *Career choice and development* (4th ed., pp. 149–205). San Francisco, CA: Jossey-Bass.

Savickas, M. L. (2005). The theory and practice of career construction. In S. D. Brown & R. W. Lent (Eds.), *Career development and counseling: Putting theory and research to work* (pp. 42–70). Hoboken, NJ: John Wiley & Sons.

Smith, R. A. (2011). *Pay for Play: A History of Big-time College Athletic Reform*. Urbana, IL: University of Illinois Press.

Super, D. E. (1957). *The Psychology of Career: An Introduction to Vocation Development*. New York, NY: Harper and Rowe.

Chapter Two

Contemporary Context of Athletics in Higher Education

Intercollegiate athletics have been woven into the fabric of higher education in the United States since the 1850s. The complicated relationship between athletics and higher education continues to evolve to this day, under the influence of institutions, media, culture, and student-athletes themselves. The largest of the governing bodies, the NCAA, formed in 1906, and has grown in stature to become more or less synonymous with college sports today (Smith, 2011). While the NCAA lacked power to enforce rules or other norms of practice and play in its early years, its power and influence grew as its membership increased. Consequently, the NCAA developed into the United States' premier governing body for college athletics in the 1950s, a full century after college athletics first surfaced at universities in the US. That dominance has persisted to this day in membership, competition, and the lucrative business side of athletics on broadcast and cable television. The NCAA, however, is not the only college sport governing body.

The National Association of Intercollegiate Athletics (NAIA) is a governing body whose tagline is "The Experts in the Business of Small College Athletics" (NAIA.org, 2018). It was founded in 1940 and grew out of the National Association for Intercollegiate Basketball (NAIB). There are currently 250 NAIA member institutions serving 65,000 student-athletes (NAIA.org, 2018). NAIA members include both public and private institutions, and span a variety of institution types such as Texas A&M-Texarkana and Indiana University-Kokomo (public), Huston-Tillotson and Dillard University (private Historically Black College/Universities), and Mid-America Nazarene University (private). The NAIA has made significant strides in fostering diversity, equity, and inclusion in intercollegiate sport. In 1948, it was the first national intercollegiate athletic organization to include African-American student-athletes in post-season play. In 1953, the NAIA invited HBCUs to become members. By 1980, it became the second governing body to sponsor intercollegiate championships for women across a range of sports (NAIA.org, 2018).

Intercollegiate athletics at the two-year level also have long-standing oversight organizations. The primary governing body for two-year institutions is the National Junior College Athletic Association (NJCAA). The NJCAA is organized into three divisions of competitiveness, each of which enforces different regulations with respect to support, travel, and scholarship money for student-athletes (Division I: full athletic scholarships, Division II: limited athletic scholarships, Division III: no athletic scholarships) (NJCAA, 2018, "Divisional Structure," para. 4). In this way, the NJCAA organizational model mirrors the NCAA in significant ways. Under the NJCAA, the country is divided into 24 geographical regions. Individual institutions are assigned to a region, and regions are represented by two appointed directors at the national level. As of August 1, 2018, the NJCAA introduced a Board of Regents above the regional directors to provide a direct link to the organization's national office (NJCAA, 2018). Within the organization's new governance structure, the Board of Regents will have a chair, woman senior administrator, man senior administrator, 24 regional representatives, six presidents, and at-large delegates as needed (NJCAA, 2018). There are currently 525 member institutions in the NJCAA.

THE NCAA

The most prominent and recognizable governing body in intercollegiate athletics is the NCAA, which boasts over 1,200 institutions serving approximately 460,000 student-athletes (NCAA.org, 2018g). Its prominence is due to a number of significant factors including longevity, the high level of play (particularly in Division I competition), the positioning of college sports and teams as cultural touchstones in general, the capital and cachet of top-tier institutions' participation, and the successful inroads NCAA competitions have made in major media markets. The NCAA has found great success in promoting competition across its sports, teams, and institutions—but it has been, perhaps, even more successful at doing so while turning a healthy profit.

The modern NCAA divisional structure was instituted in 1973 (NCAA.org, 2018g, "Historical Outline of Divisional Classification"). Its basic organizational structure is the division, and the specific rules and regulations that institutions must follow are determined by divisional affiliation. Members of each division must follow specific guidelines governing many aspects of delivering an athletic program—both on and off of the field. NCAA Division I rules, for example, require institutions to field a minimum of seven men's and seven women's sports, with two team sports for each gender (NCAA.org, 2018h). There are further guidelines for scheduling, class attendance and academic requirements for competition, and very specific regulations concerning the type and amount of athletic scholarships that can be offered to student-athletes.

More specifically, current rules allow institutions to offer two basic types of scholarship. Each depends on which sports students participate in, and the minimum and maximum amounts institutions can offer individual student-athletes is tightly regulated. The first, called equivalency scholarships, provide coaches with flexibility to divide a set number of scholarships into partial awards that can be spread out over an entire team. In other words, the coach is provided a set amount of scholarship money, and is then given the discretion to distribute the award as he or she sees fit. This can be useful in recruitment and when building a program or team. The second, known as head count scholarships, consists of full scholarships designated for each student-athlete on a qualifying team. In this case, all athletes on the team receive the same award. Typically, teams such as football, basketball, and volleyball are head count sports, whereas golf and baseball are equivalency sports. To date, legislation allows for multi-year scholarships, but institutions are not required to provide athletic scholarships beyond an annual basis.

Within Division I, institutions are further organized into subdivisions based on their football programs. The FBS fields teams at the highest level of competition and resources. The next level is the FCS, which requires less stringent attendance requirements for its football contests. There are also Division I institutions that do not field a football team (e.g., University of the Pacific). In Division I, there are over 350 member institutions offering opportunities for approximately 170,000 student-athletes (NCAA, 2018h).

Division II regulations employ a different philosophy to sport administration, and its approach reflects an understanding that while its institutions support competitive college sports programming, they do so with less financial investment (NCAA.org, 2018, "About NCAA Division II"). There are over 300 institutions within Division II supporting over 120,000 student-athletes. These institutions each must offer at least five sports for men and five for women, and field at least two team sports per gender (Irick, 2017). Division II institutions are able to offer scholarships for athletes up to the maximum amount of aid offered by each institution, including tuition, room, and board (NCAA.org, 2018e, "Division differences"). Division II also features three institutions in Puerto Rico and the only international member in the NCAA, Simon Fraser University in Canada (NCAA.org, 2018e, "What makes Division II unique").

In contrast to Divisions I and II, Division III is barred from offering athletic scholarships of any kind to its student-athletes. There are currently over 450 institutions in Division III, providing athletic opportunities for over 180,000 student-athletes (NCAA.org., 2018f, "NCAA Division III"). Student-athletes at Division III institutions are often involved in their sports in ways analogous to how students might be involved in an organization or club on campus. Division III has the same sport requirements as Division II, and must field at least five men's and five women's teams with at least two team sports sponsored for each gender.

NCAA GOVERNANCE

The NCAA is overseen at the highest level by a board of governors consisting of 20 members who represent all three divisions, including representatives spread across each of the different Division I categories (FBS, FCS, DI-No Football). The majority of members on this board of governors are college presidents, but it also includes several athletic directors (ADs) and a chancellor (NCAA, 2018a). Twenty members of the board are required to be "chief executive officers" of member institutions (NCAA, 2018a). In 2019, the NCAA added five independent board members from outside of college athletics and higher education (Bauer-Wolf, 2019). The board has oversight of areas including the NCAA's budget, strategic plan, litigation, and the annual conference. The board's charge is to ensure integrity of the national office, the collegiate model, in operating with the highest ethical standards, and in fiscal responsibility (NCAA, 2018a). Each division also has its own student-athlete advisory committee (SAAC) and governance structure. An SAAC is a group of student-athlete representatives who serve as leaders, and there are committees at the campus, divisional, and national levels (NCAA, n.d.). In 2014, the Board of Governors voted to grant autonomy to five conferences known as the Power 5 (ACC, Big Ten, Big 12, Pac-12, and the SEC). As a result, these conferences are able to develop, vote on, and implement legislation specific to the students at their institutions. There are a lot of committees in the governance structure by division. This governance structure involves students, faculty, staff, and administrators at member institutions so changes are truly member-driven.

Division I

In 1994, Division I began a movement toward "full presidential control," a process leading to the structure in place today (Smith, 2011, p. 178). Under this system, rather than giving each institution a vote in proceedings, the conferences were given power to select representatives. As a result, rather than having faculty representatives dominate committees as they had for almost a century, they were replaced by presidents and chancellors who had been selected by the conferences (Smith, 2011). Today, Division I has a board of directors with 24 members: 20 presidents or chancellors, one AD, one senior woman administrator (SWA), one faculty athletics representative (FAR), and one student-athlete (NCAA, 2019). Representatives are selected through a nomination and voting process. All FBS conferences have a president or chancellor representative, whereas the other categories of Division I (FCS, DI-No Football) are not afforded sufficient seats to represent each of their conferences. Much of the activity of the board revolves around legislation—monitoring it, preparing for future changes as issues in college athletics arise, deciding to ratify, amend, or defeat legislation—as well as supervising and monitoring the infractions process (NCAA, 2019). The Board of Directors liaises with a 32-member Presidential Forum, the Committee of Infractions, and the Infractions Appeals Committee (NCAA, 2019).

The next level of administration below the Board of Directors is the Division I Council which, according to the NCAA (2018b), "is a high-level group responsible for day-to-day decision-making" (para. 1). The council comprises 40 members including athletics administrators, FARs, and student-athletes. Each conference is represented on the council, and at least 60% of the membership must be ADs (NCAA, 2018b). The make-up of this group is intended to give more representation from racial and gender minorities (NCAA, 2018a). Much of the council's work is delegated and reviewed by the Division I board of directors. Council votes are weighted: The Power 5 representatives can cast four votes each, the FBS Group of 5 (American Athletic Conference, Conference USA, Mid-American Conference, Mountain West, Sun Belt) can each cast two votes. The remaining 22 Division I conferences receive one vote each (NCAA, 2018a). Another major administrative group alongside the council is the Division I Presidential Forum, which includes a president or chancellor from each of the 32 Division I conferences (NCAA.org., 2018c, "Division I Presidential Forum"). The 20-member Committee on Academics reports to both the Board of Directors and the Division I Council (NCAA, 2018a).

The Division I Council has several important committees that report to it: the ten-member Strategic Vision and Planning Committee, the 19-member Competition Oversight Committee, the 12-member Men's Basketball Oversight Committee, the 12-member Women's Basketball Oversight Committee, the 12-member Football Oversight Committee, and the 19-Member Legislative Committee. Each of these committees oversees reporting committees related to their main focus, and each have a student representative on them (NCAA, 2018a).

Division II

In contrast to Division I's board of directors, the primary administrative body in Division II is a group called the Presidents Council. The Presidents Council's representation is derived from the geographical regions, with one president or chancellor representing "every 22 institutions in that region," plus two at-large positions, totaling 16 representatives (NCAA, 2018b, p. 25). According to the NCAA (2018e):

> The Council's composition is based on a weighted regional representation that includes one president or chancellor per region for every 22 institutions in that region. In addition, two "at-large" positions exist to help achieve diversity of representation and to accommodate independent institutions.
>
> (para. 2)

The council oversees strategic planning, policy development, policy implementation, and budget development and approval, among other duties. It is the "Division's ultimate authority on legislation, policy and strategic direction" (NCAA, 2018d, "Division II Committees," para. 2.)

Division II also employs a 29-member Management Council which includes representatives from each of the division's multisport voting conferences, one representing independent institutions when six or more exist, two at-large positions, and two student members (NCAA, 2018b). This council interprets bylaws, organizes a Division II SAAC summit, and makes recommendations to the Presidents Council. It handles more daily responsibilities whereas the Presidents Council tends to operate at a more conceptual and oversight-oriented role. Several committees report to the Management Council: the 10-member Academic Requirements Committee, the 12-member Championships Committee, the 7-member Committee on Infractions, the 5-member Committee for Legislative Relief, the 6-member Committee on Student-Athlete Reinstatement, the five-member Infractions Appeals Committee, the 12-member Legislation Committee, the 12-member Membership Committee, the 11-member Nominating Committee, and the 29-member SAAC (NCAA, 2018b).

Division III

Division III operates in many ways like Division II, with a Presidents Council and a Management Council. The Presidents Council, with 18 members, follows specific guidelines with respect to its membership representation which is based on institutional sizes and types, as well as gender and ethnicity (NCAA, 2018c). The Management Council has 21 members, including presidents/chancellors, athletic administrators, conference representatives, and students. Like the Presidents Council, the Management Council must follow stringent rules when determining its make-up (NCAA, 2018c). These rules include at least three ethnic minorities, at least eight men and at least eight women, and at least two representations from each geographical region (NCAA, 2018c). Similar to the other divisions' committees, the Presidents Council is more conceptual in its oversight, with the Management Council handling most day-to-day operations. The following committees report to the Management Council: the 9-member Championships Committee, the 12-member Financial Aid Committee, the 5-member Committee on Infractions, the 5-member Infractions Appeals Committee, the 8-member Interpretations and Legislation Committee, the 10-member Membership Committee, the 8-member Nominating Committee, the 13-member Strategic Planning and Finance Committee, the SAAC (whose size depends on the number of Division III conferences), and the 6-member Committee on Student-Athlete Reinstatement.

GROWING STUDENT-ATHLETE POWER

With such a complex governance structure—including the Board of Governors, the divisional committees, and a range of specific committees for areas like infractions and rules of the game, with significant differences across sports—it can be difficult to identify just who has the power. For their part, even though SAACs are in place at each division and a few students have a seat at the table of the various governance committees, it has become increasingly evident that the power student-athletes wield in NCAA governance originates from outside the formal administrative structure. The time management legislation, and subsequent changes that went into effect for Power 5 institutions in fall 2017, provide an illustrative example of how student-athlete voices gained power from outside the formal structures and rose to a loud chorus of voices far exceeding the numbers on sanctioned committees. Pressure from the student voices ultimately forced changes in the NCAA time management policies (this set of events will be discussed in this chapter's section on the student-athlete experience).

While professional athletes and activism have a long and intertwined history in the United States, it has been only in the last few decades that student-athlete activism has emerged as a powerful driver of change in college sport. In 2014, for example, after several years of stalled efforts, Northwestern University's football team made a substantive push toward unionization. In a case that attracted worldwide attention and became a cultural touchstone across the United States, the student-athletes' petition was reviewed and deemed credible by the National Labor Relations Board (NLRB)'s regional director (Staurowsky, 2014). The initial win created a positive trajectory and significant momentum toward athlete unionization, and student-athletes in private institutions were declared to be institutional employees for the purposes of labor regulations. The regional NLRB's initial ruling was later dismissed by the NLRB, which did not feel it had appropriate jurisdiction to make a decision on student labor (Strauss, 2015). Northwestern's quarterback, Kain Colter, who led the efforts, was named to *The Chronicle of Higher Education*'s 2014 Influence List (Wolverton, 2014). His advocacy, in turn, inspired many other college athletes to take action on a range of issues, some focused primarily on student-athletes, others not.

Another notable and recent display of activism occurred at the University of Missouri in the fall of 2015. Student-led protests and hunger strikes were initiated in response to racial tensions at the institution, which themselves were triggered and etched into relief by the shooting of Michael Brown by a White police officer in Ferguson, Missouri. The University of Missouri's predominantly Black football team joined and escalated protests by refusing to play an upcoming football game against Brigham Young University (BYU) unless university administration resigned. Contemporary estimates suggested that forfeiting the game would have cost the university around $1 million, and the athletes' pressure eventually proved successful. The president and chancellor bowed to the student-athletes' demands and resigned (Son & Madhani, 2015). It was not until the football team joined the protests that pressure on administrators and the university's board of curators increased and became overwhelming. This was due, in no small part, to the overwhelming attention the media focused on the players.

In a related incident from earlier in 2015, University of Oklahoma football team protested a racially charged video that had been produced by a prominent fraternity. The team, which descended onto the field of play locked arm in arm and wore black in a stark symbol of protest, garnered national attention (Trotter, 2015). Recent history is full of examples showing the growing confidence and ability student-athletes have in wielding their (newfound) power to bring attention to campus and societal issues, to bend leaders and decision-makers to their will, and foster change.

Of course, for athletes and athlete-driven issues to receive attention, it is necessary for the media to play a major role. The NCAA generates most of its revenue from its Division I basketball tournament (known as March Madness), and the majority comes from TV revenue. Each conference negotiates its own TV contracts to broadcast competitions, and the sports network ESPN is the dominant media force on the college sports broadcasting scene. Not only does it broadcast games on ESPN and ABC channels, but the organization has also developed conference- and in some cases institution-focused networks with 24/7 programming for the most dedicated fans. TV contracts today are unimaginably in the billions of dollars. In 2017, the Big Ten Conference signed TV deals worth $2.64 billion (Ourand & Smith, 2017)! With television and bowl game revenue, the SEC was able to give each of its institutions almost $41 million in payouts in 2018 (Kirshner, 2018).

As media have expanded to meet the demand for hours upon hours of programming across multiple channels and networks, producers have begun to cover far more than just the competitions themselves. Today's TV lineups include pre- and post-game analysis, biopics, and interviews with coaches, staff, and players both past and present. Production values in the media space are typically high. The coin of the realm has rapidly become narratives that connect with viewers, especially those that touch upon, engage with, and provide entry into issues of the day, whether they be directly related to sports, athletes, or student-athlete activism—especially on issues of high cultural valence. Still, though media titans have been clearly focused on attracting eyeballs, driving clicks, generating likes, mentions, and hashtags, a substantial side effect of their frank monetization of all aspects of college sport is that student-athletes have gained significant clout and influence.

TRADITIONAL POWER AND INFLUENCE

While student-athletes have without a doubt seen their power and influence grow, it is important to remember that traditional sources of power and influence, including people and roles, structures, and alliances persist—and are still the primary movers and shakers in intercollegiate athletics. Drawing on his experiences as Chair of the NCAA Board of Governors from 2014 to 2016, Washington State University President Kirk Schulz suggested that NCAA President Mark Emmert, the President of ESPN, and each of the commissioners of the Power 5 conferences are the most powerful figures in college athletics today (Schulz, personal communication, February 4, 2016). Still, he acknowledged, those who govern college sports are not necessarily the same as those who wield the most influence. There are presidents at many colleges and universities who—despite leading institutions with teams that are significant players in NCAA competition—are just not knowledgeable about college athletics. Furthermore, building such knowledge can involve a steep learning curve (Woodhouse, 2015). Schulz warned that some presidents do not take the time to research issues that they vote on, and defer to commissioners' interests and desires (personal communication, February 4, 2016). It is concerning when the power to vote on issues that can substantially impact student-athletes' experiences rests in potentially uninterested or unknowledgeable presidents.

CONFERENCE REALIGNMENT

Conference realignment, or the shifting of institutions from one competition group to another, has been rampant in the past decade, and there is no better reason than money for institutions to move. Historically, conferences were organized primarily by region or institutional type (Kramer, 2016). Over time, however, traditional rivalries and regional competitions have been de-emphasized or eliminated in the pursuit of lucrative payoffs. This phenomenon has been most apparent in Division I, though numerous institutions have moved to Division II in order to increase the relative athletic talent and competition of their teams. For example, the Big 12 Conference initially consisted of two divisions and 12 institutions (hence its namesake). The original group included Baylor, Colorado, Iowa State, Kansas, Kansas State, Missouri, Nebraska, Oklahoma, Oklahoma State, Texas, Texas A&M, and Texas Tech. Over time, the group saw the development of traditional rivalries between institutions such as Nebraska and Oklahoma, or Kansas and Missouri. In the early 2010s, however, several institutions from the Big 12 opted to change conferences. Nebraska went to the Big Ten, Texas A&M and Missouri moved to the SEC, and Colorado joined the PAC-12. The Big 12 invited Texas Christian from the Mountain West Conference and West Virginia from the Big East to join; despite recruitment efforts to further expand, however, the conference currently has only ten institutions.

When conferences expand, they gain access to additional media markets in the regional areas that house the new institutions. Additional media access leads to more exposure and money. This can be very lucrative, and the additional exposure, according to Kramer (2016), also opens up new pools of talent, and can aid teams' recruitment efforts. Another reason institutions choose to realign is to "increase athletic and academic prestige" (Kramer, 2016, p. 364). While the pecuniary, competitive, and prestige advantages some institutions can gain from making a switch are attractive, the benefits are not equally distributed among all stakeholders. Redesigned conferences can mean longer travel times for many athletes. The premium on new and non-overlapping media markets translates into distances within conferences that are typically significantly farther than before (e.g., the Big Ten stretches from Lincoln, NE to New Brunswick, NJ; the Big 12 stretches from Waco, TX to Morgantown, WV). The increased distance not only inequitably increases travel expenses for smaller programs, but also results in more time away from home and school, as well as more missed classes for athletes to handle while in season. Likewise, coaches, trainers, staff, and other team personnel must spend additional time away from home and their families.

These kinds of considerations are likely not at the forefront of decision-makers' realignment plans when millions of dollars are at stake, nor when the revenue sports (e.g., football, men's and women's basketball) are scheduled by the broadcasters to maximize viewers and advertising money. It is perhaps unsurprising that competition schedules are often announced with little notice, and certainly without input from athletes. Despite the media exposure and money funneling to conference institutions, not every Olympic sport team in the Power 5 can afford to fly to every competition. As a result, students are often put in the position of making a difficult decision while weighing priorities and commitments: should they elect to miss more classes, travel further, win, and generate revenue? Or, should they push back or take a stand against a system that clearly does not prioritize their educational attainment?

ROLE OF ATHLETIC DEPARTMENTS

Athletic departments are the central administrative units tasked with managing almost every aspect of intercollegiate athletics in institutions of higher education. While they can follow several different organizational models, they serve as the conduit between institutions at large, campus units, and the professional entities that are involved in administering athletics. For example, the AD at Vanderbilt University is a tenured law professor, holds a second title of Vice Chancellor for Athletics and University Affairs, and serves within the President's Cabinet. The University of Florida and Kansas State University's athletic departments are completely separate entities from other institutional administrative units, but their ADs serve on the President's Cabinet. Across a variety of organizational structures, one clear commonality is that the AD has a direct line to the president at many universities.

An important question, then, is "do athletic departments' missions align with their colleges' missions?" Oregon State University's mission statement is, "As a land grant institution committed to teaching, research and outreach and engagement, Oregon State University promotes economic, social, cultural, and environmental progress for the people of Oregon, the nation and the world" (Oregon State University Board of Trustees, 2018, para. 2). The mission statement of Oregon State Athletics (2018), in contrast, states, "Through the power of sport, we help people discover and pursue their passions, talents and purpose in order to live a life of balance and positive contribution" (para. 2). It is clear that the two statements lack perfect alignment; Oregon State's overall institutional mission is not directed solely at developing students or specific groups of people, and the athletic department's mission is not focused on the community and Oregon. However, both mission statements convey a sense that both experiences, attending the university and participating in athletics, will contribute to students' becoming positive and productive citizens.

ROLE OF INSTITUTIONS

The institutions that offer varsity athletic programs have their own set of obligations to the student-athletes enrolled. According to Sharp and Sheilly (2008), it is paramount for colleges and universities to provide a "meaningful education" in exchange for their time and efforts in the athletic realm (p. 104). If athletes are practicing or competing during class times, there should be differentiated course time offerings so student-athletes are not excluded from pursuing certain majors based on class availability. Advisors also have an ethical obligation to encourage student-athletes to pursue the degree of their choice to avoid academic clustering, discussed in the following chapter. Given that there are many negative stereotypes of student-athletes in the classroom (e.g., Sharp & Sheilly, 2008; Simons, Bosworth, Fujita, & Jensen, 2007), colleges must have fair policies in place for student-athletes who need to miss class for athletic obligations. Though faculty have the freedom to set course policies, student-athletes should not necessarily be penalized based on assumptions of their academic abilities, especially when representing the institution in their sport.

Sharp and Sheilly (2008) suggested that "faculty should be educated about the time demands and pressures that all student-athletes experience" (p. 110). The FAR can assist in mediating any concerns between student-athletes, faculty, and the athletic department. Sharp and Sheilly (2008) encouraged a connection between the SAAC and student government to facilitate some understanding and less isolation in part by athlete-driven leadership. They also advocated for institutions to provide appropriate support programs for student-athletes, including career development, life skills, and academic support that serve athletes beyond the regular work hours and in places where student-athletes congregate (Sharp & Sheilly, 2008).

IMPACTS OF COLLEGE ATHLETES AND ATHLETICS PROGRAMS ON COLLEGES AND UNIVERSITIES

Student-athletes and college sports receive an outsized amount of media attention, despite their often small numbers on some college campuses. In Division I institutions, the number of student-athletes ranges from between

300 and 1,000 in total. At large public institutions, this could amount to less than 2% of the overall student population. Yet, colleges and universities are often known for their colors, mascots, fight songs, and athletic prominence because of their student-athletes' efforts on fields and courts. Winning teams tend to bring more attention to institutions, which may increase applications or interest from prospective students; they also tend to garner interest from donors and alumni who want to relive their (glorious) college days, or to simply associate with a winning player, team, organization, or institution. For successful programs that manage to bring in revenue, there can be significant financial benefits to the institution. Those programs may operate solely on their own budgets without taking money from student fees or institutional budgets, and may even contribute funds back to the institution. Savvy institutional decision-makers, however, tend to view the financial benefits of winning teams with cautious skepticism, as they have more often than not been proven temporary due to a phenomenon known as the "Flutie Effect." Named for quarterback Doug Flutie, who threw a game-winning Hail Mary pass for Boston College in 1984, the phenomenon is associated with increased enrollments and recruitment after a team experiences a particularly successful game or season. According to Chung (2013), athletic success might bring in more applicants, but the students attracted to institutions for this reason often tend to exhibit lower academic abilities as well.

Depending on the institution, student-athletes may also have the effect of enhancing the diversity of the student population, in particular if coaches recruit students from a variety of backgrounds and countries. While this can be seen as a positive benefit from an institutional perspective, the lived experience may be quite challenging for student-athletes who may feel doubly like a minority on campus. Athletic departments have grown increasingly aware of the struggles minority student-athletes face, especially considering that many of the major sports programs are at Predominantly White Institutions (PWIs). Several athletics programs, such as the one at Kansas State University (KSU), have launched diversity and inclusion initiatives. These efforts are overseen by a committee that includes coaches, staff from the athletic department, and KSU's FAR. The initiative offers programs for minority, first-generation, and international student-athletes; a service abroad trip for student-athletes; training and educational programs for athletic staff, coaches, administrators, and student-athletes; a committee that brings together administrators, coaches, staff, and student-athletes of color to discuss issues; and a group organized to empower female student-athletes, staff, coaches, and administrators, all focused on providing opportunities for professional and personal development (K-State Athletics, 2018).

SUMMARY

There are different sport governing bodies that are organized to operate college athletics today. The NJCAA is the primary governing body for two-year college athletics. The NAIA and NCAA serve most four-year institutions as governing bodies. NCAA governance, at the very basic level, starts with the student-athletes. Each NCAA institution has a SAAC that is a body of representatives from each varsity athletic program. The athletic conferences also have governance structures in place that involve students, athletic administrators, and academic representatives. At the national level, involvement comes from these three groups as well, including from leadership in the president and chancellor roles and from faculty members. The NCAA emphasizes that it is made up of its membership and legislation is brought forth and voted upon by its voting members. Ultimately, there is a process that reaches multiple levels of governance to make change.

The next chapter will expand upon the student-athlete collegiate experience, its opportunities and challenges.

REFERENCES

Bauer-Wolf, J. (2019, January 25). NCAA adds five independent governing board members. *Inside Higher Education*. Retrieved from www.insidehighered.com/quicktakes/2019/01/25/ncaa-adds-five-independent-governing-board-members

Chung, D. J. (2013). The dynamic advertising effect of collegiate athletics. *Marketing Science, 32*(5), 679–698.

Irick, E. (2017). *Student-athlete participation 1981–82–2016–17: NCAA sport sponsorship and participation rates report*. Indianapolis, IN: NCAA.

Kirshner, A. (2018, February 2). The SSEC is paying out a record $40.9 billion per school and the Big Ten could pass it soon. Retrieved from www.sbnation.com/college-football/2018/2/2/16964186/sec-revenue-distribution-2017

Kramer, D. A. II. (2016). Motivations to switch: Refuting the public discourse on athletic conference realignment. *The Review of Higher Education, 39*(3), 339–370.

K-State Athletics. (2018). *Diversity & inclusion*. Retrieved from www.kstatesports.com/sports/2017/8/23/diversity-inclusion.aspx

NAIA.org. (2018). National Association of Intercollegiate Athletics. Retrieved from www.naia.org

National Collegiate Athletic Association (NCAA). (2016). *GOALs study of the student-athlete experience: Initial summary of findings*. Indianapolis, IN.

National Collegiate Athletic Association (NCAA). (2018a). *Division I manual*. Indianapolis, IN.

National Collegiate Athletic Association (NCAA). (2018b). *Division II manual*. Indianapolis, IN.

National Collegiate Athletic Association (NCAA). (2018c). *Division III manual*. Indianapolis, IN.

NCAA. (2019). *NCAA division I board of directors*. Retrieved from www.ncaa.org/governance/committees/division-i-board-directors

NCAA.org. (n.d.). *NCAA student-athlete advisory committees (SAAC)*. Retrieved from www.ncaa.org/about/resources/media-center/news/conferences-refer-time-demands-proposals-further-study

NCAA.org. (2018a). *About NCAA Division II*. Retrieved from www.ncaa.org/about?division=d2

NCAA.org. (2018b). *Division I Council*. Retrieved from www.ncaa.org/governance/committees/division-i-council

NCAA.org. (2018c). *Division I Presidential Forum*. Retrieved from www.ncaa.org/governance/committees/division-i-presidential-forum

NCAA.org. (2018d). *Division II Committees*. Retrieved from www.ncaa.org/governance/committees?division=d2

NCAA.org. (2018e). *Division II Presidents Council*. Retrieved from www.ncaa.org/governance/committees/division-ii-presidents-council

NCAA.org. (2018f). *Division III Management Council*. Retrieved from web1.ncaa.org/committees/committees_roster.jps?CommitteeName=3MC

NCAA.org. (2018g). *Divisional Differences and the History of Multidivisional Classification*. Retrieved from www.ncaa.org/about/who-we-are/membership/divisional-differences-and-history-multidivision-classification

NCAA.org. (2018h). *NCAA Division I*. Retrieved from www.ncaa.org/about?division=d1

NJCAA.org. (2018). *Divisional structure*. Retrieved from www.njcaa.org/member_colleges/Divisional_Structure

Oregon State Athletics. (2018). *Mission statement*. Retrieved from http://osubeavers.com/sports/2009/4/30/208343856.aspx

Oregon State University Board of Trustees. (2018). *Oregon State University mission statement*. Retrieved from https://leadership.oregonstate.edu/trustees/oregon-state-university-mission-statement

Ourand, J., & Smith, M. (2017, July 25). Big Ten formally announces new rights deals through '23 with ESPN, Fox, CBS. *Sports Business Daily*. Retrieved from www.sportsbusinessdaily.com/Daily/Issues/2017/07/25/Media/Big-Ten.aspx?printandclose=true

Sharp, L. A., & Sheilly, H. K. (2008). The institution's obligations to athletes. *New Directions for Higher Education*, 142, 103–113.

Simons, H. D., Bosworth, C., Fujita, S., & Jensen, M. (2007). The athlete stigma in higher education. *College Student Journal*, 41(2), 251–273.

Smith, R. A. (2011). *Pay for Play: A History of Big-time College Athletic Reform*. Urbana, IL: University of Illinois Press.

Son, C., & Madhani, A. (2015, November 9). Missouri president, chancellor quit after football team walks out. *USA Today*. Retrieved from www.usatoday.com/story/news/2015/11/09/mizzou-faculty-walks-out-student-association-calls-presidents-removal/75448392/

Staurowsky, E. J. (2014). An analysis of Northwestern University's denial of rights to and recognition of college football labor. *Journal of Intercollegiate Sport*, 7, 134–142.

Strauss, B. (2015, August 17). N.L.R.B. rejects Northwestern football players' union bid. *New York Times*. Retrieved from https://nytimes.com/2015/08/18/sports/ncaafootball/nlrb-says-northwestern-football-players-cannot-unionize.html

Trotter, J. (2015, December 28). Protests, adversity build OU's team chemistry. Retrieved from www.espn.com/college-football/story/_/id/14449290/behind-oklahoma-sooners-bond-forged-racist-video-protest-last-spring

Wolverton, B. (2014, December 15). 2014 influence list: Athletes' advocate. *The Chronicle of Higher Education*. Retrieved from www.chronicle.com/article/Athletes-Advocate-Kain/150849

Woodhouse, K. (2015, April 16). NCAA novices. Retrieved from www.insidehighered.com/news/2015/04/16/some-presidents-face-steep-learning-curve-athletics

Chapter Three

The Student-Athlete Experience
Opportunities and Challenges

THE STUDENT-ATHLETE EXPERIENCE

Student-athletes have a rare and unique opportunity to represent an institution in competition at a high level. Their experience of playing the dual student and athlete roles is distinctive, and comes with a unique set of opportunities and challenges. Together, those create a bond of common experience among student-athletes across divisions and at all levels of competition. At some Division III institutions, large numbers of enrolled students participate in varsity-level athletics, whereas at Division I institutions only a small percentage of the student population participates in elite college sports. Division III and Ivy League coaches recruit students for their athletic talents despite the inability to offer athletic scholarships (Harrison & Lawrence, 2003). Even so, these young people make up the largest number of NCAA athletes (Harrison & Lawrence, 2003). Division III institutions offer their students some of the strongest athletic traditions, rivalries, and travel opportunities to rigorous competitions; understandably, there is no shortage of young students who are willing to compete at the Division III level.

Despite Division II and Division III student-athletes comprising the vast majority of the overall student-athlete population, the spotlight and media attention paid to Division I student-athletes has fostered popular belief that the Division I student-athlete experience, as portrayed in popular culture and the media, is the norm. This belief is reinforced by extended, though often skewed, visibility in the media, as the general public is likely only exposed to Division I athletic teams through television broadcasts of competitions and discussions during the news hour by sportscasters. The public may know that their favorite competitors are indeed college students, but that reality is subordinated by the well-reinforced and powerful narratives that are portrayed when they see the athletes participate in competitions on TV or, on occasion, in person. At the very core, each student-athlete—whether in the NCAA divisions, NAIA, NJCAA, or at institutions under other governing bodies—has a unique, individual experience in college. Every institution will offer a student a different college experience, and have various levels of resources and program offerings to shape their development.

Time Demands

In 2015, the NCAA conducted what is called the Growth, Opportunities, Aspirations and Learning of Students in College (GOALS) study. The findings revealed startling information about the student-athlete experience, in particular with respect to time commitments necessary to participate in the full range of athletic-related activities. The NCAA (2016) found that student-athletes' time devoted to athletic pursuits had increased since its previous study in 2010. Football programs in Division I (FBS and FCS) averaged about 40 hours a week in athletic-related activities, and some other sports averaged just under that. The results showed that the median time spent on athletic activities was 34 hours per week in Division I, 32 hours per week in Division II, and 28.5 hours per week in Division III (NCAA, 2016). Considering the amount of time students were also spending on academics (38.5 hours per week in Divisions I and II, and 40.5 hours per week in Division III), it would be easy to conclude that there appears to be a lack of balance between what amounts to two full-time roles: college student and elite athlete.

As a follow-up to the GOALS study results, the NCAA (2016) conducted a more extensive and focused time demands study, collecting data from 44,058 Division I athletes as well as from more than 5,000 athletic administrators and coaches. The ensuing report (NCAA, 2003) highlighted areas of consensus and suggestions for change to current policies governing time commitment for athletic-related activities. The suggestions from the report included observing an eight-hour overnight break between athletic-related activities, instituting a two-week no-activity period at the end of competition season, and providing a rest period between returning home from travel after competition before the next practice or competition. All were adopted by the Power 5 conferences and implemented in the fall of 2017 (NCAA, 2003). The GOALS study in 2015 was sponsored by the Division I SAAC, from which student voices spurred the process of change (Hosick, 2016).

Pressure to Perform

Since the 1950s, NCAA Division I intercollegiate athletics has emerged as a multimillion-dollar business operating within institutions of higher education (Lapchick, 2006). The increasingly lucrative partnerships and opportunities they create have posed challenges, not only for Division I institutions but also for student-athletes. For their part, colleges and universities must offer quality educational experiences that support student development, provide academic enrichment, and prepare students for future careers. At the same time, they must do so in a system and environment that is often pressured to privilege the growing big-business side of athletic departments, at the expense of developmental, academic, and career priorities (Thelin, 1994). While challenges vary across divisions and from institution to institution, the pressures of commercialization characteristic of many Division IA (now FBS) intercollegiate athletic departments are a real and growing problem (Croissant, 2001).

These institutional challenges put Division I student-athletes in an unenviable position of being at the epicenter of potentially conflicting missions: while navigating the tension between their competing roles as student or athlete, the priorities they make can make or break the success of the business model (Danish, Petitpas, & Hale, 1993). Moreover, since the turn of the century, coaches and athletics administrators have faced increasing pressure to deliver winning teams in what has become an indisputably commercialized system (Croissant, 2001). As student-athletes try to balance dual full-time roles of student and athlete, the emphasis by coaches, the media, and the university community pushes athletes to focus more on their athletic identity (Adler & Adler, 1991). It is in this environment that student-athletes have often struggled to successfully prepare for a future outside the world of athletics while simultaneously performing as winning elite athletes (Danish et al., 1993; Miller & Kerr, 2003).

MYTHS ABOUT THE STUDENT-ATHLETE EXPERIENCE

Despite their popularity and acceptance in the media, public assumptions—including on campus—about athletes have traditionally been based on stereotypes. The "dumb jock" myth, for example, though dating back to the mid-1960s, still permeates academia, causing some students, faculty, and staff to view student-athletes as undeserving of a place in college. Research (e.g., Simons, Bosworth, Fujita, & Jensen, 2007) has indicated that many faculty members have negative perceptions about student-athletes, though emerging research has shown that such perceptions tend to be directed primarily toward football players (Kuhn, 2017). Student-athletes are often seen as big stars on campus who receive advantages both within and outside of the classroom (Adler & Adler, 1991). In reality, however, student-athletes can experience significant isolation from the rest of campus, even if they want to just be "regular students" (Rubin & Moses, 2017).

Perceptions are further shaped and hardened when people see student-athletes receiving free gear, meals, and travel opportunities, creating ample opportunity for some to question the fairness of the arrangements institutions make to support their players. Many of the perceptions, however, are based on a superficial and incomplete understanding of the context. As was revealed by the NCAA's time demand studies, in addition to time dedicated to their athletic pursuits, student-athletes are often required to participate in a range of community service, along with other institutional and student development activities. With few other options available, they may need to take advantage of targeted programming offered by their athletic departments (e.g., tutoring, advising) because their schedules are simply incompatible with campus activities that are designed around "traditional" student schedules.

Students in classes with athletes may be reluctant to work with student-athletes for group projects or on other collaborations because they perceive the athletes to be unreliable or incompetent, yet that perception is likely irreconcilable with the truth: student-athletes are often among the hardest-working and most committed students on campus. Many student-athletes start their day before dawn to attend workouts, treatment sessions with athletic trainers, team and solo practice, meetings with coaches, in travel between a competition the night before in another city or state, or due to any number of other possible actions. Moreover, long after the traditional school day is complete, student-athletes may be asked or required to join coaches or school administrators for a range of university functions that further encroach upon their time. By the time student-athletes attend classes or turn toward their student responsibilities, they might be exhausted for a number of reasons. These remarkable students are always "on" in the public eye, representing the university in every aspect of their lives.

Finally, because of their highly structured schedules, student-athletes must also actively schedule study time, meals, meetings, and other obligations in ways that the general student body does not. As a result, they are not always available to meet with their peers in the evenings for group projects, study sessions, or even just to relax socially. Some coaches even impose evening curfews on student-athletes, including on the weekends and during the off season. Student-athletes also commit themselves to their institutions beyond their physical bodies, mental dedication and focus, and time. They are often called upon—explicitly and implicitly, actively and passively—to represent the university by substantially committing their identities to their athletic roles (Adler & Adler, 1991). Yet, much of the conversation surrounding the collegiate athlete experience, in particular the negative perceptions, originates with non-athletes and those who have little knowledge of college athletics. This leads to misinformation and misunderstanding about the student-athlete experience in the public at large, helps to ensure that stereotypes exist and persist, and fosters an incorrect and damaging narrative in the media and in popular culture. Much of this is avoidable and unfortunate, as athletic departments and the student-athletes representing their colleges and universities are well positioned and often empowered in a number of ways to make positive impacts on their institutions.

In the face of these substantial challenges, including stereotyping, significant time demands, and pressures to perform in an increasingly commercialized system, they must develop as whole individuals, as well as gain marketable career skills. In contrast to the typical college student, student-athletes' personal and professional development must take place both on and off the field, in a high-stakes, high-scrutiny, and high-pressure environment.

CHALLENGES AND BARRIERS TO STUDENT-ATHLETE PERSONAL AND CAREER DEVELOPMENT

Whether they participate in intercollegiate athletics or not, college students undergo intense periods of multifaceted personal development while navigating the higher education experience. As a result, the college years are often viewed as one of the most critical periods in which young adults develop a sense of identity (Brown, Glastetter-Fender, & Shelton, 2000). Brown et al.'s (2000) and Cote's (2006) research suggested that students face two main psychosocial challenges: (a) establishing a career identity; and (b) preparing for the transition to adulthood. Their works shows the higher education experience's substantial impact on how students develop, mature, and construct career identities in preparation for the real world (Brown et al., 2000; Cote, 2006). Cote (2006) further identified the transition to adulthood as a foundational period of human identity development.

Realistically, for the vast majority of intercollegiate athletes, the "real world" means choosing a career path that is not as a professional athlete. According to the NCAA's most recent study to estimate the probability of a student-athlete pursuing professional sport, less than 3% of student-athletes will eventually turn professional in their sport (NCAA, 2011). Exploring this phenomenon, Danish et al. (1993) and Murphy, Petitpas, and Brewer (1996) found that student-athletes' psychosocial struggles and experiences designing and constructing career identities can often be characterized by submission to a type of identity foreclosure. Marcia, Waterman, Matteson, Archer, and Orlofsky (1993) described identity foreclosure as an individual's process of committing to familiar or expected career fields without exploring alternatives. Research by

Blustein and Phillips (1990) further suggested that students in a state of identity foreclosure may struggle to take responsibility for making career choices. Considering student-athletes consistently blur roles as students and athletes, Good, Brewer, Petitpas, Van Raalte and Mayer (1993) and Murphy et al. (1996) have posited that they may resign themselves to careers closely associated with the sport industry due to a lack of career exploration and the tendency to gravitate toward familiar career settings. In addition, Blann (1985), Kennedy and Dimick (1987), and Sowa and Gressard (1983) suggested that student-athletes struggle to dedicate sufficient time and resources toward career and postgraduate plans. This paucity of time individuals dedicated to career exploration can result in a lower perceived level of career maturity upon graduation (Kennedy & Dimick, 1987; Sowa & Gressard, 1983). Failure to explore opportunities outside of familiar contexts requiring only comfortable skillsets can limit the career construction process and severely limit potential career choices. The genesis of these challenges for student-athletes can be traced to structures, barriers, and challenges in the student-athlete experience, both internal and external.

Internal Barriers to Personal and Career Development

Among impactful, internal, and psychosocial challenges experienced by intercollegiate athletes, role conflict, athletic identity salience, and identity foreclosure have been shown by contemporary research to be most common. As student-athletes navigate college they are likely to face internal career construction challenges rooted in or related to these internal conflicts.

Role Conflict. Student-athletes often struggle to balance competing roles as students and athletes (Adler & Adler, 1987), a finding that draws on Chickering's (1969) and Erikson's (1959) descriptions of the stages and vectors integral to the identity development process. Their work suggested that developing a stable sense of identity may be the most consequential challenge late adolescents face. The distinctive experience of the student-athlete and their struggles to form and embrace roles has sparked and increased interest in role conflict among intercollegiate athletics researchers.

Erikson's (1959) framework suggested that individuals pass through eight developmental stages, including: (a) infancy, (b) early childhood, (c) play age, (d) school age, (e) adolescence, (f) young adulthood, (g) maturity, and (h) old age. Each stage presents a psychosocial crisis that triggers a maturation process, and that identity is constructed as one endures crises. His work further suggested that individuals often develop and maintain solidarity with the norms of specific affinity groups during times of crisis (Erikson, 1959).

For his part, Chickering (1969) suggested that identity is developed as students acquire specific skills during their higher education experience. He posited seven vectors through which individuals pass and master; each influences students' development of personal identity and success in life after college. The vectors include: (a) developing competence, (b) managing emotions, (c) developing autonomy, (d) establishing identity, (e) developing mature interpersonal relationships, (f) clarifying purpose, and (g) developing integrity (Chickering 1969; Howard-Hamilton & Sina, 2001; Sowa & Gressard, 1983). The work of Chickering and others suggested that if college students master these seven skills, their chances at a successful transition from college to career fields is more likely.

Adler and Adler (1987), Chartrand and Lent (1987), and Hill, Burch-Ragan, and Yates (2001) built on these seminal theories by applying their frameworks to the student-athlete experience. Specifically, they explored the role conflict many student-athletes face during their college experience and how it impacts their identity development processes. Adler and Adler (1987) and Chartrand and Lent (1987) posit student-athletes often identify first as athletes, second as students, and often struggle to develop a well-rounded sense of identity. Hill et al. (2001) found that student-athletes identify primarily with athlete roles, leaving their student roles overshadowed and even neglected. The work of these scholars highlights how role conflict can complicate the ways student-athletes approach career development and construction during their time in college.

More recently, Meyer (2003) investigated ways that role conflict impacted career choice. Her survey work, including the Career Influences Inventory (CII), illustrated how student-athletes clearly associate with athletic identities, but in so doing fail to see their academic development as salient to their career decisions. Most student-athletes in the study rated their role as an athlete as the most influential factor in career decisions, demonstrating how role conflict can stifle meaningful career exploration.

Finch (2007) further explored the need for career development programming designed to help student-athletes associate and identify with roles other than that of "athlete." The study found that identification with a "student" role positively and significantly predicted self-efficacy in career decision-making. Identification with athletic roles, on the other hand, did not. Moreover, the results demonstrated how role conflict directly affects career planning as student-athletes who associated more with student identities expressed a greater sense of control and autonomy in the career choice process. A notable finding from the study suggested that women, overall, tended to associate more with student roles, while males participating in revenue-generating sports tended to associate more with athletic roles. While the study further highlights the impact role conflict can have on student-athletes, it further demonstrated how the effect can vary and shift within and across individuals and subpopulations.

Bell (2019) interviewed Division I football players to explore how different people in student-athletes' lives impact how they define identity. Findings suggested that coaches and athletic academic advisors had a significant influence in the likelihood to identify with the role of student. Likewise, teammates and student-athlete peers were also found to be influential as well. Though the study does not implicate a "most influential" player in the likelihood to identify with specific roles, it demonstrates the importance those surrounding student-athletes during college have in identity and career development.

Athletic Identity Salience and Identity Foreclosure. Researchers have also explored how and why student-athletes often tend to associate more with athletic roles, or possess a stronger sense of athletic identity, as such tendencies can impact the construction of viable career paths (Brown et al., 2000; Murphy et al., 1996; Snyder, 1983). Specifically, scholarship has revealed how the phenomenon known as identity foreclosure, or failure to explore and pursue career fields outside of comfortable and or known alternatives, can influence student-athletes' career construction processes.

Marcia (1966) first examined identity foreclosure as a barrier to career development, a general psychology phenomenon. She demonstrated that identity foreclosure can occur when individuals make premature career-related decisions and do not adequately explore opportunities that are available. Moreover, foreclosure can lead individuals to pursue socially acceptable roles that align with how one identifies with life roles. Marcia's work underwrites subsequent exploration of career exploration and decision-making.

Snyder (1983), in his studies of the sociology of sport, adapted and applied the concept of identity foreclosure to the student-athlete population to explore the role sport plays in one's life. He posited that an individual student-athlete's level of engagement influences self-identification with the role of athlete, that athletes experience intrinsic satisfaction from sport, as well as an endorphin high from competition, and that desire for physical exertion stimulates a feeling of self-worth. He described athletes as "active animals," motivated to perform a task with competence (Snyder, 1983, p. 99). In addition, he identified the role victories, recognition, power, and prestige play as extrinsic motivators. Taken together, the intrinsic and extrinsic satisfaction gained from participation in sport, forward the athletic identity as the most salient role.

Murphy et al. (1996) utilized the Career Maturity Inventory (CMI) to explore relationships between athletic identity and career decision-making ability, and found that athletic identity and identity foreclosure are inversely related to career maturity. Specifically, student-athletes who identified primarily as athletes often delayed career plans, and were more likely to experience difficulty making career decisions. Related work by Brown et al. (2000) explored identity foreclosure and student-athletes' expectations to "go pro." They found that most students recognized they will not become professional athletes, but many held aspirations to work in sport industries. Further student-athletes reported a lack of exposure to alternative career paths.

Researchers focusing on student-athletes have consistently demonstrated that these individuals have consistently failed to explore careers outside of sport. Due to identity foreclosure, student-athletes often commit themselves to career paths in the sport industry that are familiar and comfortable, but not necessarily optimal. The body of work in this area highlights importance for holistic programs to support student-athletes in meaningful and positive career exploration as they approach the inevitable next chapter of life after sport.

External Barriers to Academic and Career Development

Researchers have persuasively demonstrated intense internal battles that student-athletes face that affect career development during college (Adler & Adler, 1987). Others (e.g., Chartrand & Lent, 1987; Renick, 1974) have focused on external factors, including institutional barriers that also impact career exploration and development. Specifically, they identified that isolation from the student body and academic clustering affect career construction.

Isolation from the Student Body. Sport-related activities, practice, and travel often isolate student-athletes from the general student population, a reality with which institutions struggle, and one that poses important questions for the direction that student-athlete support programs should take, namely integration or isolation (Adler & Adler, 1987; Chartrand & Lent, 1987; Rubin & Moses, 2017). Work by Harris, Altekruse, and Engels (2003) examined the stress experienced by students and student-athletes who participated in small psycho-educational programming in the first year of college. Student-athletes reported greater relaxation and reduced stress when surrounded by other student-athletes. As a result, Harris et al. (2003) argued that isolation is an effective method to support student-athletes adjusting to college. Jolly (2008) also argued for targeted programs for student-athletes. His research found that separate programming allows individuals to more fully engage because they are surrounded by individuals who share common schedules and challenges. The work of Harris et al. (2003) and Jolly (2008) represented one framework and approach to programming that begins with separation, segregation, or isolation of student-athletes.

In contrast, work by Broughton and Neyer (2001), Howard-Hamilton and Sina (2001), and later Umbach, Palmer, Kuh, and Hannah (2006) argued that student-athletes should be integrated into the regular student body for support programming. Broughton and Neyer (2001) found that social isolation, faculty isolation, and even peer isolation can develop early in the college experience for student-athletes. Howard-Hamilton and Sina (2001) agreed and warned that feelings of isolation from the regular student body can have long-term effects on student-athletes' psychosocial and cognitive career development processes. Furthermore, Umbach et al. (2006) suggested that the integration of student-athletes may carry benefits, including decreased feelings of social isolation and improved developmental processes. The findings of these researchers suggest that programming should start with integration, and that support approaches should co-exist with other campus-wide initiatives.

Though these two bodies of research support vastly different approaches to supporting student-athlete development, both camps emphasize the importance of holistic well-being, (e.g., athletic, cognitive, and psychosocial development), and not merely athletic development. What their research does not directly address, however, is whether programming borne of either approach is better suited for supporting student-athletes' academic development or career construction processes. It is critical, therefore, for the student-athlete voice to be at the epicenter of attempts to examine these programs.

Academic Clustering. While commitment to one's sport and balancing dual roles of student and athlete may contribute to a lack of career exploration and choice, institutional barriers can also complicate the career construction process. Scholars such as Renick (1974), Case, Greer, and Brown (1987) and Fountain and Finley (2009, 2011) have identified a practice called "academic clustering" in which student-athletes are funneled toward certain majors, primarily to maintain eligibility. This can, in turn, lead to misalignment of career aspirations. Research conducted at Division I (especially FBS) institutions, suggested that certain student-athletes face significant barriers to obtaining meaningful academic degrees due to their participation in sport.

While Renick described academic clustering as early as 1974, Case et al. (1987) performed the first comprehensive study of clustering related to student-athletes, basketball specifically. The authors defined academic clustering as when 25% or more of the players on a given team pursued a similar major. They found not only that universities frequently cluster student-athletes in specific majors, but also that it appears more common among men's teams than female teams. In addition, they found that African-American student-athletes were more often funneled to specific majors than Caucasians.

Suggs (2003) studied academic clustering in football by looking for patterns in the majors of players on teams competing in 2002 bowl games. His findings showed that football players were concentrated in certain majors considered "athlete-friendly" or to be the path of least resistance to maintaining eligibility, and comparatively, the majors were saturated with student-athletes.

Fountain and Finley (2009) explored the practice further, with a specific focus on race. They studied Division I football players at 11 schools throughout the ACC conference. Their study turned out to be consistent with Suggs' (2003) work by revealing clustering at every school. Moreover, players who identified as minorities were clustered in specific majors more than their Caucasian teammates. Additional analysis revealed a secondary layer of clusters as well. At certain institutions, more than 50% of minority players were clustered in majors such as Sociology and Sport Management. Fountain and Finley (2011) also suggested while this practice happens with all sports, it occurs most consistently with African-American student-athletes participating in major revenue-generating sports such as basketball and football.

Overall, these studies reveal practices in which institutions engage that can significantly impact student-athletes' opportunities to explore potential career pathways, in particular Division I (mainly FBS) student-athletes. These studies, however, fail to identify who wields the most influence in the choice: student-athletes themselves or athletic departments that may be providing encouragement or even coercion. Potentially, the phenomenon is a function of both. It is therefore critical to consider student-athletes' perspectives when developing programming aimed at supporting the career choice process.

The combined impact of the internal psychosocial struggles and external institutional barriers student-athletes experience during college can lead to difficulties for individuals considering life after sport or exploring career paths (Danish et al., 1993; Fountain & Finley, 2009, 2011; Kennedy & Dimick, 1987; Sowa & Gressard, 1983; Renick, 1974). In the face of these challenges, the NCAA's stated ultimate academic goal that student-athletes graduate with meaningful degrees that prepare them for career fields in life after sport can seem ironic (Lyons, 2011). Further, these challenges persist even as institutions and athletic departments have—and will continue to develop, implement, and manage—programs with the NCAA's goal in mind, not to mention their own consonant goals as institutions of higher education. Still, the question remains: How effective are the programs institutions have developed in preparing student-athletes for life after intercollegiate sport?

EMERGING CHALLENGES FOR MILLENNIAL AND GENERATION Z STUDENT-ATHLETES

Student-athletes today are primarily members of the Millennial generation, and are now starting to come from Generation Z. Contemporary research suggests that Millennial student-athletes' challenges during transition from high school to college, and from college to career fields, are distinctive (Bell, 2009; Comeaux & Harrison, 2011; Navarro, 2015). Milkman (2017) described Millennial students as having seven defining characteristics differentiating them from previous generations. He suggested that Millennials are: (a) rule-following, (b) sheltered, (c) confident, (d) conventional, (e) team-oriented, (f) pressured, and (g) high-achieving. While challenging for Millennial students, in general, Bell (2009) suggested these characteristics can cause further difficulties for student-athletes. These special challenges, pressures of commercialized intercollegiate athletics, and the need for student-athletes to develop dual student/athlete identities together present a need for student affairs professionals to better understand the unique needs of Millennial and Gen Z student-athletes (Broughton & Neyer, 2001).

Coomes and DeBard (2004), Pizzolato, and Hicklen (2011), and Odenweller, Booth-Butterfield, and Weber (2014) have explored ways Millennial students, because they are unlike previous generations, pose significant challenges to current student development program models and student affairs, academic affairs, and athletics affairs practitioners today. They described Millennials as ambitious, but directionless; as possessing an innate need to achieve, but an inadequate competence for how to do so independently—especially in relation to their Baby Boomer parents (Pizzolato & Hicklen, 2011). Levine and Dean (2012) and Odenweller et al. (2014) further posited that Boomer parents engage in excessive preemptive problem-solving that has robbed their children of opportunities to learn even basic independent analysis or conflict resolution strategies. They are by no means cognitively impaired, but have under-developed independence needed to navigate college successfully. Coomes and DeBard (2004) also emphasized Millennial students' desire to conform in order to reduce external pressure.

Gen Z students are extraordinarily dependent on technology, and this impacts how they digest learning. Because of this technology-driven world they grew up in, Gen Z athletes "require increased stimulation" from coaches and educators (Parker et al., 2012, p. 7). They are considered digital natives (Levine & Dean, 2012; Rickes, 2016). Gen Z-ers grew up watching Shark Tank for inspiration rather than cartoons. They expect to be communicated with via social media or online in some way (e-mail being seemingly outdated) (Spears, Zobac, Spillane, & Thomas, 2015)! Fewer Gen Z athletes are viewing sport participation as fun in their youth; rather, they are interested in being competitive and advancing their skills (Parker et al., 2012) or consider it a health tool (Elmore, 2014). Parker et al. (2012) found in their study of Gen Z youth soccer players that the participants appreciated when coaches are knowledgeable about and skilled in their sport. They also discovered that athletes find it important to participate in team decision-making, which indicates a thirst for leadership development (Parker et al., 2012). This, of course, is an opportunity for student-athlete development professionals to consider when designing leadership development programming and opportunities for participation.

The Gen Z students emphasize the importance of social justice (Boleska, 2018; Hope, 2016) and sustainability (Rickes, 2016), and represent a highly diverse group (Levine & Dean, 2012). Currently, Gen Z makes up more than a fourth of the United States population, and "will become more global in their thinking" than Millennials (Boleska, 2018, p. 10). Gen Z students are also seeking immersive experiences, aiming to leave a mark on the world without recognition (Boleska, 2018). The fact that both Millennial and Gen Z students are globally focused and new college students are motivated for social justice action and initiatives means there are opportunities to offer student-athlete study abroad and service trips, which are truly immersive experiential opportunities. These programs will be discussed further in the next chapter.

Current literature reveals evidence that the student-athlete experience is unique from that of the regular college student. Researchers who have studied the student-athlete undergraduate experience (e.g., Baillie & Danish, 1992; Chartrand & Lent, 1987; Gaston-Gayles & Hu, 2009) suggested that the unique challenges student-athletes face negatively influence their levels of campus-wide engagement and holistic development during college. While these pressures have always impacted student-athletes, they can be more pronounced for Millennial and Gen Z student-athletes, even more so for those at the Division I level for whom student development programming is most often provided in isolation from the general population (Bell, 2009). This new generation of student-athletes is, incredibly, the most connected to people through technology yet more isolated than ever because of it (Levine & Dean, 2012), requiring both independent time for learning and collaborative environments (Seemiller & Grace, 2016).

Student affairs practitioners, for their part, are charged with the difficult job of assisting this unique population, and have followed a range of strategies and approaches to support student-athletes during college and beyond. Yet, there has been a recent and growing recognition that many of those approaches may not be as effective for Millennial and Gen Z student-athletes (Adler & Adler, 1987, Baillie & Danish, 1992, Broughton & Neyer, 2003; Harrison & Lawrence, 2003). New external influences, such as multimillion-dollar television contracts, have become an accelerant to the commercialization of college sport, increasing the pressure on coaches and athletics administrators to produce winning teams (Croissant, 2001). Also, there is a challenge with Millennials' tendency to need the coddling they received from their parents while in college, whereas Gen Z-ers are more independent (Rickes, 2016).

For their part, media forums have continued to depict large Division I athletic departments as systems which exploit student-athletes for their athletic prowess, but place little emphasis on meaningful career development for athletes post-college and post-sport (Fountain & Finley, 2011; Renick, 1974; Suggs, 2003; Thelin, 1994). These researchers' findings suggest that the commercialization of intercollegiate athletics has led to a perception that an undergraduate degree is merely a commodity to maintain eligibility, rather than a vehicle to prepare student-athletes for meaningful careers in life after sport. Also, many students in Generation Z are unconvinced that a college education has value when there are entrepreneurial ways to be successful at their fingertips, and NCAA regulations may restrict these activities while they compete as student-athletes (Hope, 2016). Another way to engage Gen Z students who are enterprising and creative is with the makerspace (Rickes, 2016). These are modern, technology-enhanced "craftshops" that engage students to be creative through their learning (Rickes, 2016, p. 32). In this creative spirit, Gen Z students tend to learn through more kinesthetic, hands-on experiences that apply knowledge to an act of doing (Shatto & Erwin, 2016). Their attention spans are limited when it comes to attending lectures, speakers, and workshops. Student affairs professionals need to incorporate interactive activities and even students' phones in learning activities and programs (Shatto & Erwin, 2016).

While these issues may be most pronounced for Millennial and Gen Z student-athletes who participate in mainstream sports at the Division I level, similar issues exist across divisions. According to Levine and Dean (2012) and Elmore (2014), this upcoming generation is facing a dismal economy after being raised in a recession, coupled with unrealistic expectations for the future. These students do not necessarily understand that, when entering the workforce, they have to work their way up to earn supervisory roles and salaries above entry level. Millennials are considered people who are comfortable spending money with abandon whereas those in Generation Z prefer to save money (Elmore, 2014; Hope, 2016). This is important as financial literacy programming must be tailored to student-athletes based on their personal financial behaviors. As a result, the ways institutions provide support to their student-athletes for life after college has become a critical question for student and academic affairs professionals.

The NCAA's (2011) study to investigate the probability of a student-athlete becoming a professional athlete estimated that, on average, less than 3% of those competing at the intercollegiate level will "go pro." This suggests, at the very least, that the overwhelming majority of student-athletes need assistance developing career prospects other than professional sport. This can be a difficult task given the enhanced pressure student-athletes experience from multiple spheres of influence (e.g., parents, coaches, faculty) (Gaston-Gayles & Hu, 2009). To this end, contemporary student affairs professionals who work with student-athletes must consider and address additional challenges as they must work to balance the pressures and future needs of Millennial and Gen Z student-athletes. Spears et al. (2015) found that when studying Gen Z students' participation in a face-to-face learning community, they preferred to interact with peers (student employees) who engaged them through social media and in teaching. This presents an opportunity for student-athlete services professionals to incorporate peer-run programs (e.g., senior athlete leaders who mentor junior athletes).

Gen Z students also crave face-to-face interaction, but in a way, they are conditioned to communicate online instead. Therefore, their interpersonal skills and oral communication skills are lacking (Seemiller & Grace, 2016). Since they prefer to communicate more with shorthand and symbols than complete sentences, written communication can also be a challenge, which makes writing assignments a challenge (Elmore, 2014). Student-athlete services professionals might also have to focus on communication skills development with their students, as employers are seeking graduates who have both professional oral and written communication abilities (NACE, 2018).

RELEVANT THEORETICAL FRAMEWORKS

Theoretical frameworks inform both research and practice concerning student-athletes in their academic and personal pursuits while in college. Several theories have risen to prominence in student-athlete affairs, and are highlighted here for use in developing or examining programs meant to support this distinctive population.

Mindset

Mindset theory was developed by Dweck (2006), who studied how students and educators view intelligence. Decades spent studying children in the classroom informed the theory which posits that individuals have one of two types of mindset: fixed or growth. Individuals with a fixed mindset believe that one is born with fixed intelligence and cannot become smarter. People with a fixed mindset can become frustrated if they do not know an answer or struggle to solve a problem. They might even lie about their progress to avoid feeling less intelligent. In contrast, individuals with a growth mindset believe they need only put forth effort to learn, and by doing so, have the ability to grow in intelligence.

Individuals do not necessarily possess the same mindset about every aspect of life. For example, a student-athlete might have a growth mindset with respect to athletic ability, and therefore practices and continues to perform in the hope of improving over time. The same individual, however, might exhibit a fixed mindset with respect to academic pursuits, rather than seeing potential to strengthen performance in both domains. Dweck's work (2006) resulted in a simple four-question assessment that can be used to estimate students' mindsets. Professionals working with athletes incorporate this theory in practice with students, especially to reveal to them that they are growth-oriented in athletics, yet hold a fixed mindset concerning their studies.

Identity Development

Chickering and Reisser (1993) authored a theory of identity development for college students which describes the process as spanning seven vectors (stages of development), including: developing competence, managing emotions, moving through autonomy toward interdependence, developing mature interpersonal relationships, establishing identity, developing purpose, and developing integrity. Valentine and Taub (1999) explored application of the theory to student-athletes. They found that in relation to the first vector, competence, student-athletes must often contend with the "dumb jock" stereotype as they develop academic skills. In response, support professionals often provide proactive support related to competence to keep the tension from negatively affecting student-athletes. At the same time, student-athletes tend to exhibit high physical competence. This can be positive for their development unless facing injury, which can cause identity struggles. Student-athletes may also struggle to develop interpersonal competence as their interactions with other students may be limited due to their athletic time commitments (Valentine & Taub, 1999).

Valentine and Taub (1999) noted that the competitive nature of sports' highs and lows, wins and losses, as well as the aggressive nature of some competition may impact how student-athletes learn to manage emotions, the second vector in Chickering and Reisser's (1993) theory. The third vector, moving through autonomy toward interdependence, can present a challenge for athletes, who often have a relatively highly structured higher education experience characterized by management and direction from coaches in the athletic sphere, and from both faculty and support professionals in academics. With limited time for extracurricular activities, assuming ownership and responsibility for decision-making concerning academics and personal development can be difficult (Valentine & Taub, 1999). Similar time management concerns affect the fourth vector, developing mature interpersonal relationships. While student-athletes may form close relationships with players and coaches in the context of their teams, they may not have the same opportunities to do so on campus.

Establishing identity can be a turning-point vector for student-athletes as it involves a variety of components:

- comfort with body and appearance, comfort with gender and sexual orientation,
- sense of self in relation to one's social and cultural context,
- clarification of self-concept through roles and lifestyle,
- sense of self in response to feedback from valued others,
- self-acceptance and self-esteem, and
- personal stability and integration.

(Valentine & Taub, 1999, p. 171)

Each of the vectors presents student-athletes with multifaceted challenges including physical fitness, eating disorders, and substance abuse. Homophobia permeates many aspects of athletic culture, which can turn sexual orientation and gender identity into a minefield of development challenges. Popular culture is rife with stereotypes about athletes based on race, gender, sexual orientation, nationality, and other profile characteristics which can make establishing a stable, healthy identity a monumental task for student-athletes unsure about themselves. Valentine and Taub (1999) also warn that some student-athletes "may have internalized the 'dumb jock' image that some of their peers and professors hold of them" (p. 173).

The developing purpose vector is where student-athletes can potentially experience identity foreclosure as individuals struggle to look beyond college to future career possibilities. This can be of particular difficulty for some student-athletes who have never identified themselves as anything but athlete for most of their lives. They might also be

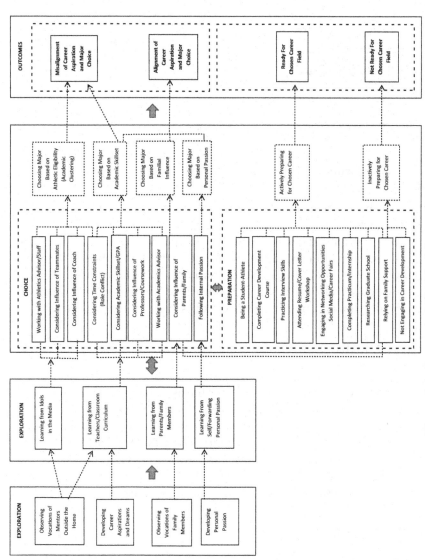

Figure 3.1 Conceptual Model of Career Construction

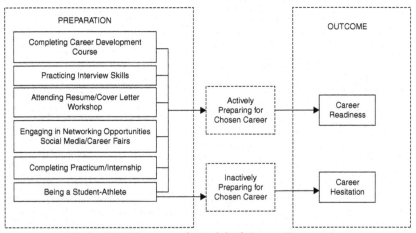

Figure 3.2 Conceptual Model of Career Preparation

considerably more invested in their athletic role than in their academic role in college.

Developing integrity, the final vector, incorporates "developing personal values and then bringing behavior in line with those values" (Valentine & Taub, 1999, p. 176). For student-athletes who have followed rigid structures and rules that have been provided and enforced throughout college, developing a personal code of ethics can be difficult to achieve.

Career Construction

Navarro (2015) developed models of student-athletes' career construction and career preparation as they plan for life after sport (see Figure 3.1 and Figure 3.2). Her interviews with student-athletes about their career exploration, career choice, and career planning revealed tensions between their academic and athletic roles and identity struggles. Her work emphasized the importance of implementing intentional career development initiatives for student-athletes, as well as of engaging athletes with campus career development offerings.

REFERENCES

Adler, P., & Adler, P. (1987). Role conflict and identity salience: College athletics and the academic role. *Social Science Journal*, 24(2), 443–450.

Adler, P., & Adler, P. A. (1991). *Backboards and Blackboards: College Athletes and Role Engulfment.* New York, NY: Columbia University Press.

Baillie, P. H. F., & Danish, S. J. (1992). Understanding the career transition of athletes. *The Sport Psychologist, 6*, 77–98.

Bell, L. F. (2009). Examining academic role-set influence on the student-athlete experience. *Journal of Issues in Intercollegiate Athletics*, Special Issue, 19–41.

Blann, F. W. (1985). Intercollegiate athletic competition and students' educational and career plans. *Journal of College Student Personnel, 26*(2), 115–118.

Blustein, D. L., & Phillips, S. D. (1990). Relationship between ego identity statuses and decision-making styles. *Journal of Counseling Psychology, 37*, 160–168.

Boleska, K. (2018). *Motivations of NCAA student athletes in community service* (Unpublished doctoral dissertation). University of the Incarnate Word, San Antonio, TX.

Brewer, B. W., Van Raalte, J. L., & Linder, D. E. (1993). Athletic identity: Hercules' muscle or Achilles heel? *International Journal of Sport Psychology, 24*, 237–254.

Broughton, E., & Neyer, M. (2001). Advising and counseling student athletes: New *Directions for Student Services*, 93(Spring), 47–53.

Brown, C., Glastetter-Fender, C, & Shelton, M. (2000). Psychosocial identity and career control in college student-athletes. *Journal of Vocational Behavior, 56*, 53–62.

Case, B., Greer, S., & Brown, J. (1987). Academic clustering in athletics: Myth or reality? *Arena Review, 11*(2), 48–56.

Chartrand, J. M., & Lent, R. W. (1987). Sports counseling: Enhancing the development of the student-athlete. *Journal of Counseling and Development, 66*(4), 164–167.

Chickering, A. W. (1969). *Education and Identity*. San Francisco, CA: Jossey-Bass.

Chickering, A. W., & Reisser, L. (1993). *Education and Identity*. San Francisco, CA: Jossey-Bass.

Comeaux, E., & Harrison, C. K. (2011). A conceptual model of academic success for student-athletes. Educational Researcher, 40(5), 235–245. https://doi.org/10.3102/0013189X11415260

Coomes, M. D., & DeBard, R. (Eds.). (2004). Serving the Millennial generation: New Directions for Student Services, 106.

Cote, J. E. (2006). Emerging adulthood as an institutionalized moratorium: Risks and benefits to identity formation. In J. J. Arnett & J. L. Tanner (Eds.), *Emerging adults in America: Coming of age in the 21st Century* (pp. 85–116). Washington, DC: APA.

Croissant, J. L. (2001). Can this campus be bought? Commercial influence in unfamiliar places. *Academe, 87*(5), 44–48.

Danish, S. J., Petitpas, A. J, & Hale, B. D. (1993). Life development intervention for athletes: Life skills through sports. *Counseling Psychologist, 21*(3), 352–385.

Dweck, C. S. (2006). *Mindset: The New Psychology of Success.* New York, NY: Random House.

Elmore, T. (2014, August 15). How Generation Z differs from Generation Y [Blog post]. Retrieved from https://growingleaders.com/blog/generation-z-differs-generation-y

Erickson, E. (1959). Identity and the life cycle: Selected papers. *Psychological Issues, 1*(1), 5165.

Finch, B. L. (2007). Investigating college athletes' role identities and career development. (Doctoral dissertation, Texas A & M University). Retrieved from ProQuest (Publication No. 3281057).

Fountain, J. J., & Finley, P. S. (2009). Academic majors of upperclassmen football players in the Atlantic Coast Conference: An analysis of academic clustering comparing white and minority players. *Journal of Issues in Intercollegiate Athletics, 2,* 1–13.

Fountain, J. J., & Finley, P. S. (2011). Academic clustering: A longitudinal analysis of Division I football programs. *Journal of Issues in Intercollegiate Athletics, 4,* 24–21.

Gaston Gayles, J., & Hu, S. (2009). The influence of student engagement and sport participation on college outcomes among Division I student athletes. *Journal of Higher Education, 80*(3), 315–333.

Good, A. J., Brewer, B. W., Petitpas, A. J., Van Raalte, J. L., & Mayer, M. T. (1993). Identity foreclosure, athletic identity, and college sport participation. *The Academic Athletic Journal,* Spring, 1–12.

Harris, H. L., Altekruse, M. K., & Engels, D. W. (2003). Helping freshman student athletes adjust to college life using psychoeducational groups. *Journal for Specialists in Group Work, 28*(1), 64–81.

Harrison, C. K., & Lawrence, S. M. (2003). African American student athletes' perceptions of career transition in sport: A qualitative and visual elicitation. *Race, Ethnicity and Education, 6*(4), 373–394.

Hill, K., Burch-Ragan, K., & Yates, D. Y. (2001). Current and future issues and trends facing student athletes and athletic programs: *New Directions for Student Services,* 93, 65–80.

Hope, J. (2016). Get your campus ready for Generation Z. *Dean and Provost, 17*(8), 1–7.

Hosick, M. B. (2016, August 15). Conferences refer time demands proposals for further study. Retrieved from www.ncaa.org/about/resources/media-center/news/conferences-refer-time-demands-proposals-further-study

Howard-Hamilton, M. F., & Sina, J. A. (2001). How college affects student athletes: New Directions for Student Services, (*93*)1, 35–45.

Jolly, J. C. (2008). Raising the question #9: Is the student-athlete population unique? And why should we care? *Communication Education*, *57*(1), 145–151.

Kennedy, S. R., & Dimick, K. M. (1987). Career maturity and professional sports expectations of college football and basketball players. *Journal of College Student Personnel*, *27*, 548–559.

Kuhn, A. P. (2017). *Faculty perceptions of student-athlete deviance: A SEC and Big Ten comparison* (Doctoral dissertation). Retrieved from ProQuest (10754683)

Lapchick, R. E. (2006). *New Game Plan for College Sport*. Westport, CT: Praeger Publishers.

Levine, A., & Dean, D. R. (2012). *Generation on a Tightrope: A Portrait of Today's College Student*. San Francisco, CA: Jossey-Bass.

Lyons, J. (2011). The NCAA is redefining the student-athlete. Retrieved October 15, 2011 from http://education-portal.com/articles/NCAA_is_Redefining_the_Student-Athlete.html

Marcia, J. E. (1966). Development and validation of ego identity statuses. *Journal of Personality and Social Psychology*, *3*, 551–558.

Meyer, K. J. (2003). *Influences on career decisions of college student-athletes*. (Unpublished Master's thesis). Northwestern University, Evanston, IL.

Milkman, R. (2017). A new political generation: Millennials and the post-2008 wave of protest. *American Sociological Review*, 82(1), 1–31. https://doi.org/10.1177/0003122416681031

Miller, P. S., & Kerr, G. A. (2003). The role experimentation of intercollegiate student athletes. *The Sport Psychologist*, 17, 196–219.

Murphy, G. M., Petitpas, A. J., & Brewer, B. W. (1996). Identity foreclosure, athletic identity, and career maturity in intercollegiate athletes. *The Sport Psychologist*, 10, 239–246.

National Association of Colleges and Employers (NACE). (2018, February 19). Are college graduates "career ready"? [Blog post]. Retrieved from www.naceweb.org/career-readiness/competencies/are-college-graduates-career-ready

Navarro, K. M. (2015). Preparation for life after sport. In E. Comeaux (Ed.), *Making the connection: Data-informed practices in academic support centers for college athletes* (pp. 91–108). Charlotte, NC: Information Age Publishing.

NCAA (2003). *CHAMPS/Life Skills Program.* Retrieved from www.ncaa.org/wps/ncaa?key=/ncaa/NCAA/Academics+and+Athletes/CHAMPS+ +Life+Skills/Program

NCAA. (2011). *Estimated probability of competing in athletics beyond the high school interscholastic level.* Retrieved from www.ncaa.org/wps/wcm/connect/public/NCAA/Issues/Recruiting/Probability+of+Going+Pro

Marcia, J. E., Waterman, A. S., Matteson, D. R., Archer, S. L & Orlofsky, J. L. (1993). *Ego Identity: A Handbook for Psychosocial Research.* New York: Springer-Verlag.

Odenweller, K. G., Booth-Butterfield, M., & Weber, K. (2014). Investigating helicopter parenting, family environments, and relational outcomes for Millennials. *Communication Studies, 65*(4), 407–425.

Parker, K., Czech, D., Burdette, T., Stewart, J., Biber, D., Easton, L., ... McDaniel, T. (2012). The preferred coaching styles of Generation Z athletes: A qualitative study. *Journal of Coaching Education, 5*(2), 5–23.

Pizzolato, J. E., & Hicklen, S. (2011). Parent involvement: Investigating the parent–child relationship in millennial college students. *Journal of College Student Development, 52*(6), 671–686.

Renick, J. (1974). The use and misuse of college athletics. *The Journal of Higher Education, 45*(7), 545–552.

Rickes, P. C. (2016). Generations in flux: How Gen Z will continue to transform higher education space. *Planning for Higher Education Journal, 44*(4), 21–45.

Rubin, L. M., & Moses, R. A. (2017). Athletic subculture within student-athlete academic centers. *Sociology of Sport Journal, 34*(4), 317–328. doi:10.1123/ssj.2016-0138

Seemiller, C., & Grace, M. (2016). *Generation Z Goes to College.* San Francisco, CA: Jossey-Bass.

Shatto, B., & Erwin, K. (2016). Moving on from millennials: Preparing for Generation Z. *Journal of Continuing Education in Nursing, 47*(6), 253–254.

Simons, H. D., Bosworth, C., Fujita, S., & Jensen, M. (2007). The athlete stigma in higher education. *College Student Journal,* 41, 251–273.

Snyder, E. E. (1983). Identity, commitment, and type of sport roles. *Quest, 35*(2), 97–106. doi: 10.1080/00336297.1983.10483787

Sowa, C., & Gressard, C. (1983). Athletic participation: Its relationship to student development. *Journal of College Student Personnel,* 24, 236–239.

Spears, J., Zobac, S. R., Spillane, A., & Thomas, S. (2015). Marketing learning communities to Generation Z: The importance of face-to-face interaction in a digitally driven world. *Learning Communities Research and Practice, 3*(1), 1–10.

Suggs, W. (2003). Jock majors: Many colleges allow football players to take the easy way out. *The Chronicle of Higher Education, 49*(17), 33.

Thelin, J. R. (1994). *Games Colleges Play: Scandal and Reform in Intercollegiate Athletics.* Baltimore: John Hopkins University Press.

Umbach, P. D., Palmer, M. M., Kuh, G. D., & Hannah, S. J. (2006). Intercollegiate athletes and effective educational practices: Winning combination or losing effort? *Research in Higher Education, 47*(6), 709–733.

Valentine, J. J., & Taub, D. J. (1999). Responding to the developmental needs of student athletes. *Journal of College Counseling, 2*(2), 164–179.

Chapter Four

Programs That Support Student-Athletes

Higher education leaders, athletic administrators, scholars, and the NCAA have come to the shared conclusion that student-athletes, like other distinctive student groups, need targeted support to help maximize success, both on and off the field. In addition to the media attention and scrutiny student-athletes face, the identity struggles and progression to life after sport continues to bring targeted support to the forefront. While individual institutions and their athletic departments have, for decades, developed programs to address student-athletes' needs, there was a growing recognition in the late 1980s that a more directed and standardized approach was warranted. As a result, the NCAA debated a slate of new proposals to address a range of student-athlete needs. In 1991, landmark legislation was adopted that fundamentally changed the face of student-athlete programming, as well as the responsibilities and relationships between student-athletes, athletic departments, and the institutions at which they studied. Language included in the legislation set the groundwork for contemporary approaches to the programs that support student-athletes today. That initial legislation applied only to Division I institutions, but in subsequent years, similar regulations were passed to cover Division II and III institutions. Today all NCAA institutions must follow some version of the legislations, though there are significant differences in language and requirements between divisions.

A critical component of the initial legislation was section 16.3.1, which makes it *mandatory* for Division I institutions to offer academic counseling and support services (16.3.1.1) as well as life skills programs (16.3.1.2) to all student-athletes (Comeaux, 2015; NCAA, 2018). In other words, the legislation required that NCAA member institutions must newly fund a range of programs and services to support student-athletes, including filling new staff positions to fulfill these roles. Importantly, the legislation was explicitly worded such that "…counseling and tutoring services may be provided by the department of athletics or the institution's nonathletics students support services" (NCAA, 2018, p. 224). This seemingly minor distinction concerning who or where on campus support services originate has, in subsequent years, grown into a substantive distinction in how programming is administered, can be classified, and interpreted. This has also led to a significant shift in the structure of the academic and student-athlete development units nationally. Beginning in the early 2000s, departmental shifts began as academic support units operated separately from divisions of student-athlete development. With this came the addition of jobs focused solely on the career, personal, and leadership development of student-athletes. In the last five years, departments have continued to focus on growth of positions solely dedicated to student-athlete development. However, legislation still does not exist consistently across divisions.

The Division II language of section 16.3.1 (adopted in 2004), also required institutions to provide financial support for a range of support services, including tutoring expenses and professional sports career counseling. While the legislation required institutions to fund diverse approaches to supporting student-athletes, its list of permissible activities notably (and explicitly) forbade institutions from funding computers if they were designated solely for student-athletes (NCAA, 2018).

A full 17 years after the original Division I legislation was passed, the NCAA in 2008 developed and passed language that applied to Division III member institutions. The Division III version of the 16.3 legislation is broken up into four areas (NCAA, 2018): Section 16.3.1 outlines rules governing the types of academic-based programming institutions are permitted to finance so long as similar options are made available to all students. Section 16.3.2 covers support services and other programming that other students can generally access unrelated to athletic participation (e.g., leadership programming, career development) unless a team is in season, making athletic-related programming specifically for athletes allowable. The 16.3.3 language permits institutions to financially support SAAC meetings, including those requiring travel. Finally, Section 16.3.4 outlines rules permitting institutions to fund life skills programming as long as those programs are generally available to non-athletes as well.

While the NCAA legislation was in many ways quite prescriptive about the types of programming that should be offered, to whom it should be offered, and in what contexts, it did not specifically outline requirements for budgets, staffing, facilities, expertise, reporting structures, or degree of creativity in offerings. As a result, since the legislation's passage within each division, member institutions have interpreted the legislation broadly, and have developed a diverse range of support programs, specialized positions, elaborate facilities, and both unique and distinctive opportunities to support student-athlete development. Likewise, institutions have explored a range of approaches to funding their programs, often demonstrating (or flouting) their commitment to the mandate along the way. Specifically, programs continue to exist in various forms under multiple titles and divisions. The student development side of these support services have names such as student-athlete affairs, student-athlete development, student-athlete enhancement, life skills, and leadership development.

Position titles and structures also vary. At many institutions (e.g., Kansas State University, University of Washington), these programs are part of the same unit that houses athletic academic advising. At other institutions (e.g., Florida State University, University of Nebraska), they are separate units within the athletic department. Some of the units may encompass areas beyond what was initially focused on five pillars of CHAMPS, the initial NCAA life skills program, which was launched in 1994 (NCAA, n.d.-b). These five pillars were personal development, career development, community service, athletic excellence, and academic excellence (Vanderbilt University, n.d.). While these five areas are still part of the student-athlete development programming offered today, the NCAA is no longer overseeing professional development for those who work in this field. The N4A now leads professional development for student-athlete development/life skills professionals (Leach, 2015).

The remainder of this chapter provides examples of support programs offered across today's intercollegiate athletics landscape, describes common components and structures to those programs, highlights promising and effective practices, and points to distinctive models designed to support specific aspects of student-athlete development.

ACADEMIC SUPPORT PROGRAM DESIGN AND EXAMPLES

Depending on the type and size of institution, the governing body/division in which the institutions sits, the importance of athletics in the institution's culture, and the level of resources leadership commits, academic support programs for athletes can differ significantly from institution to institution. These differences can manifest in a variety of ways. Some institutions build and manage substantial facilities solely for the student-athlete population; others do not. Some employ advisors to work exclusively with student-athletes; others hire generalists to work with both athletes and non-athletes. Some institutions house and administer support services for athletes separately from the rest of campus; at others, such units report to the provost through academic affairs, and/or are part of a centralized advising model serving the general student population. Likewise, there are instances in which athletic support units report 50% to athletics and 50%

to academic affairs, among other percentage splits. Points of comparison among these programs, as well as contrasts, are numerous.

Despite their critical role in supporting student-athletes, there has been limited research on the effectiveness of different program models. The paucity is, in part, because research across programs is especially difficult given the diversity of models, structures, and funding levels across institutions. Complicating matters further, as individual institutions field different numbers of sports and enroll vastly different numbers of athletes, it is unclear whether identifying a one-size-fits-all program is even practical or possible. This is especially true when attempting to make comparison across different divisions, conferences, or the different sport governing bodies' members.

NCAA Division I

NCAA Division I encompasses a wide variety of institutions that can be categorized in numerous ways. This diversity includes institutions with comparatively large and wealthy athletic programs such as those in the Power 5 conferences, institutions in the so-called (and for some, pejoratively named) "mid-major" conferences, low-resource institutions, and minority-serving institutions. Despite significant differences within and across Division I support programs, however, these institutions and the approaches they develop and implement set the tone for what is and can be done across the NCAA as a whole. The tendency for administrations across the NCAA to look to Division I institutions for successful support models has both pros and cons. In implementing the best programs, building the best facilities, and promoting the best results, well-resourced institutions can provide an example for others looking to support their own athletes. At the same time, the impressive work they do may only be possible due to the resources available, and smaller, lower-resource institutions may struggle to match the implementation.

HBCUs. Many HBCUs are classified as low-resource institutions and have limited student-athlete services staff. In recognition of these challenges, the NCAA offers support for these institutions through its Accelerated Academic Success Program (AASP). The AASP offers grants to support low-resource institutions at two levels: comprehensive (multi-year) or initiative (single-year) grants. Comprehensive grants provide up to $300,000 per year for up to three years, which may be used for hiring academics staff, offering summer financial aid for student-athletes, developing summer bridge/mentoring/tutoring programs, or improving technology (NCAA, 2018). Initiative grants provide up to $100,000 for one year and may be used to update facilities, upgrade technology, create career development programming for students, and hire part-time staff such as graduate assistants and tutors (NCAA, 2018a).

While these NCAA grants can help institutions launch new, or improve existing, programming, only small numbers of institutions receive such supplemental funding. Still, all NCAA members, including HBCUs, must provide programming. Cooper (2015) examined academic support programs for athletes at HBCUs, and noted a number of common approaches and practices:

> A review of these data-driven studies reveals five common strategies implemented by HBCUs and their academic support staff that have facilitated positive outcomes for their student-athletes: a) early intervention programs, b) purposefully designed study halls, c) institution wide academic support services, d) public recognition of student athletes' academic achievement, and e) nurturing familial campus climates.
>
> (p. 66)

It is important to note that programmatic approaches grow out of the context in which they sit. The practices revealed in Cooper's (2015) study of HBCUs support students by establishing environments characterized by familial support and relationships. This finding is consistent with other research on HBCUs (Hirt, Amelink, McFeeters, & Strayhorn, 2008; Palmer & Gasman, 2008), but may or may not find similar success in other contexts.

Other Divisions and Governing Bodies

Outside of Division I, variation in practices increases further. While NCAA Division II athletics programs may provide dedicated support professionals and facilities for their student-athletes, the resources committed to athletes are seldom offered at the same level as Division I institutions. As a result, programs at these institutions are more likely to be offered to student-athletes alongside and integrated with the rest of the student population. In other words, there is seldom specialized or targeted programming or advising for student-athletes

Likewise, as NCAA Division III and NAIA institutions do not fund scholarships for athletes, institutional culture and programming instead focus on the holistic college experience; participation in athletics is often seen as extracurricular. At NJCAA institutions, some student-athletes may have been awarded an athletic scholarship, and may need assistance to navigate the process of transfer from a two- to a four-year institution. In response, NJCAA institutions may commit an academic support professional to work with athletes as part of their duties, in either a full-time or part-time capacity. It is not uncommon for academic support professionals at two-year institutions to be experts in NAIA rules as well as NCAA rules across all divisions. This expertise arises because the student-athletes they support likely have no idea where they will transfer, if and when they are recruited. They must remain eligible and ready, and their institutions' student-athlete support professionals help them navigate the complex NCAA regulations.

SPECIFIC PROGRAMMING MODELS

Programs that support student-athletes in higher education are diverse, and the ways individual programs develop can be impacted by a variety of factors including NCAA division, the role that athletics plays at the institution, institution size, focus, funding, and more. Despite that diversity, the overall goal of these programs is to provide support, and while student-athletes are not a homogeneous group, they often have similar needs. Given that basic focus, programs typically incorporate a common set of approaches or components that have come to define contemporary student-athlete support services. Keeping in mind that scale, scope, and fidelity of implementation will depend upon place and context, as well as focus and funding, this section will highlight aspects of student-athlete support that are currently and commonly offered at many institutions.

Student-Athlete Development

Student-athlete support services typically include what the NCAA previously called "life skills," now more commonly referred to as "student-athlete development." These programs focus on the holistic development of the student, including elements of personal, character, leadership, and career development. These aspects can be achieved through programs and activities, both short-term and longitudinal in nature. In this context, "programs and activities" can be understood to include a range of optional or mandatory services in which student-athletes participate. These can include facilitated workshops, educational or training sessions, experiential learning experiences (e.g., study abroad), and access to personnel dedicated to helping student-athletes navigate challenges such as the post-college transition and employment.

Many athletic departments hire student-athlete development specialists to organize these types of programs for access during the academic career. Some programs even hire specialists to work within specific areas of focus. For example, the University of Arkansas athletic department employs its own employer relations specialist to develop athletes' job searching and employment skills as well as relationships between employers and athletes (University of Arkansas Student-Athlete Development, 2018). Still, despite the need and benefit, Navarro (2015) cautioned that similar programs should not focus solely on seniors, but instead ensure that student-athletes throughout their college experience are involved in meaningful and time-appropriate career development activities.

The growing recognition that student-athletes often need specialized career development support may help explain recent growth in these types of positions. For example, Boston University's athletic department created a new position in 2017, the Director of Leadership and Career Development (Raglin, 2017). Oregon State Athletics, in line with its mission statement introduced in Chapter 2, offers a personal and professional development program just for football players called Beyond Football (Oregon State Athletics, 2018). Due to their unique experiences in college, there has been a growing recognition of a need for dedicated staff to help student-athletes navigate life, learn valuable skills both for their college experience and for life after sport, and to provide resources to support student-athletes' overall health and well-being. Another important set of knowledge and skills for student-athletes is financial literacy, and institutions are now offering more programs and resources on financial education. As the focus of this area has recently encompassed other aspects of holistic development, such as nutrition and mental health, the area of "student-athlete enhancement" is becoming part of the nomenclature to encompass more than just the idea of student development.

Community Outreach and Engagement

Given cultural interest in sport heroes, it is perhaps unsurprising that athletic departments receive many requests from their surrounding communities to engage in service and outreach activities. While coaches can be a big draw, the presence of student-athletes is in demand for various types of organizations and schools. In response to the high demand, many athletic departments support a dedicated community outreach coordinator position that may or may not be housed with student-athlete services. Within the University of Illinois at Chicago's athletic department, for example, the community outreach coordinator is part of the marketing and tickets unit (University of Illinois at Chicago Athletics, 2018). The coordinator receives community requests for student-athlete, coach, or staff appearances, and then matches opportunities to individuals. These kinds of engagements, while certainly representing a substantial time commitment for athletes, can also be highly beneficial opportunities for developing skills like public speaking and mentoring. They can also enrich the student-athletes' networks and exposure to leadership or employment contacts. Many athletic departments pair these types of opportunities with educational opportunities to ensure that the student-athletes not only develop community outreach skills, but also represent their institutions positively outside of their sport.

Specialized Learning and Targeted Tutoring

Another recent area of growth in student-athlete support is the role of the learning specialist (Wolverton, 2016). Learning specialists work with students who may have learning disabilities, academic deficiencies, enter the institution below its academic standards, or who may struggle in classes for a range of different reasons. Some athletic departments employ one or more full-time learning specialists, some with specializations (e.g., math specialist, reading specialist). For many athletics programs, however, the cost of filling these positions is not a feasible expense, so students are referred to campus learning support.

Learning specialists and targeted tutoring approaches assist many student-athletes, but also invite criticism and controversy. For some, the critique is one of equality and equity, and arises from the general (but often uninformed) view that such support represents a privilege afforded athletes at the expense of other students. Often, the reaction is more a response to institutional spending on segregated facilities than on the service provided (Grossman, 2008; Thamel, 2006). To be sure, there are examples of institutions that invite such criticism, but there is little evidence to suggest such practices are widespread.

Another source of critique is concern that the purpose of such programs is not to support students so much as to support institutions' athletic endeavors; that support is focused primarily on doing whatever is needed (even unethically) to keep athletes eligible (Grasgreen, 2012). Critics point to NCAA waivers and other practices as eliding the underlying issues of academic performance (Farrey, 2009). Indeed, while recent years have seen bad practices uncovered at a small number of errant institutions, their poor examples should not be taken as standard operating procedure across athletics in higher education. Learning support and tutoring programs also provide student-athletes support outside of normal business hours when campus support centers are open.

Return to Learn

Another group of programs have identified and developed innovative opportunities for collaboration between seemingly disparate units across campuses to help athletes succeed in college. One such program, known around the country as Return to Learn, supports student-athletes who were diagnosed with concussion during competition by providing them with academic accommodations to ease their transition back into the classroom. This support goes beyond academic advising, as it may involve sports medicine/ athletic training, student-athlete support services, student access centers/ disability resources, academic affairs, faculty senate, a college's intercollegiate athletic council, and other units on campus. University of Minnesota's example is a model program that highlights how institutions can harness available resources to help student-athletes who are concussed.

Return to Learn Program Model: University of Minnesota. The University of Minnesota's Athletic Medicine department developed and approved a Concussion Management Plan in 2017 that incorporates several elements, including a Return to Learn policy. First, the plan emphasizes that "the health and safety of our student-athletes is the first priority of the University of Minnesota" (University of Minnesota Athletic Medicine, 2017a, p. 1). The plan requires that student-athletes, athletic department staff, and medical staff (e.g., athletic trainers and team physicians) are provided concussion education. Student-athletes receive pre-participation concussion assessments including a full review of their brain injury and concussion histories. The program includes a process for recognizing and diagnosing concussions, as well as a post-concussion management plan. The plan also outlines two different policies and procedures for Return to Play and Return to Learn (University of Minnesota Athletic Medicine, 2017a).

The Return to Learn policy was initially developed through a collaboration between Athletic Medicine and the Lindahl Academic Center staff. The language of the policy needed to be consistent with campus language for policies, so the academics staff worked with the Athletic Medicine staff to ensure it was written in a way that would be acceptable to institution stakeholders. While developing language for the policy, the authors sought the expertise of the learning specialist, who, as the liaison to the Disability Resource Center (DRC), provided information for the document. Final language was reviewed by the DRC to ensure faculty would approve. According to the learning specialist:

> It has helped limit the number of students we have had to register [with the DRC] tremendously. I think the combination of having Athletic Medicine send the document to Academics to forward out, gives the perception of a medical note from a doctor and less of Academics having to make a judgment call about what a student should and should not be doing.
>
> (S. Shuey, personal communication, January 24, 2018)

Further, the director of the Lindahl Academic Center meets each semester with the academic advisors for each college on campus to discuss the policy so advisors are aware of it and how Return to Learn works at Minnesota.

The policy outlines levels of instructional modification and academic accommodation from Level 1 (no academic activities) to Level 5 (full academic activities/no accommodations) (University of Minnesota Athletic Medicine, 2017a). The policy also includes a special note about students who are in physical education classes, requiring additional monitoring or are being held at Level 1 until cleared by the team physician. The document that the Athletic Medicine unit sends out to the academics staff is in the form of a letter entitled "Accommodations for Student-Athlete Recovering from a Concussion." The letter includes signs and symptoms of concussions, a checkbox list including the gravity of each level, as well as a check indicating the level at which the particular student-athlete is at the time. The letter also includes signs to look for after a concussion, and concludes with contact information for the student's specific athletic trainer (University of Minnesota Athletic Medicine, 2017b). Examples are shown in Figure 4.1a and b.

Mental Health and Well-Being

Issues surrounding student-athletes' mental health and well-being have long been a concern in intercollegiate athletics, but have risen recently to the forefront of discussion in college athletics (Broughton & Neyer, 2001; Pinkerton, Hinz, & Barrow, 1989). Distinctive and significant challenges arise when trying to help student-athletes who need support for mental health concerns (Yang et al., 2007). Resources for student-athletes are not always available "in-house" in the athletics facilities. Recognizing mental health as a growing issue, a handful of institutions have moved to create positions and hire mental health counselors to serve student-athlete populations on campus.

Consonant with the diversity in approaches to programming throughout athletics administration elsewhere, there is great diversity to how mental health and wellness are addressed from institution to institution. Some athletic departments make arrangements with institutional counseling centers to engage counselors to work part-time serving the athletes, but in athletic facilities where athletes already hang out. In other cases, the athletes are referred to services and facilities off campus in the community, so these easily recognized individuals will not draw attention to themselves walking into a campus counseling center.

PROGRAMS THAT SUPPORT STUDENT-ATHLETES

UNIVERSITY OF MINNESOTA - ATHLETIC MEDICINE
Accommodations for Student-Athlete Recovering from a Concussion

Today's Date

Dear University Academic Staff,

Student-Athlete has been diagnosed with a concussion on **Date of Concussion** and is currently under the care of the University of Minnesota Athletic Medicine Staff – both Team Physicians and Athletic Trainers.
Current Intercollegiate Athletics Concussion Management Plan calls for no classroom activity on the same day as a concussion injury. Full ICA Concussion Management Plan can be found at: UMN Concussion Management Plan.

Signs and Symptoms of a Concussion:	
Headache	Difficulty remembering or paying attention
Confusion	Balance problems or dizziness
Nausea or vomiting	Feeling sluggish, hazy, foggy, or groggy
Sleep problems	Feeling irritable, more emotional or "down"
Bothered by light or noise	Double or blurry vision
Slowed reaction time	Loss of consciousness

Participating in school, work, and physical activity can exacerbate these symptoms and may need to be limited or avoided altogether Student-athletes exhibiting significant symptoms should be held out of school or work until these symptoms are lessened or gone. Any activity that significantly increases symptoms should be stopped until the symptoms are resolved.

MEDICAL RECOMMENDATIONS:
Current Level of Instructional Modifications and Academic Accommodations

Student-athletes who are currently enrolled in any physical education class requiring activity participation will be withheld from participation until resolution of the injury, or as otherwise dictated by the managing Team Physician.

☐ Level 1   No Academic Activities

☐ Level 2   Limited Academic Activities-Limited Class Attendance
          MAC Counselor will advise which classes student-athlete may attend.
          Maximum Accommodations may include: limited assignments; no exams/quizzes;
          frequent breaks during class; scribe/classmate for note taking.

☐ Level 3   Moderate Academic Activities-Class Attendance to Tolerance
          MAC Counselor will advise which classes student-athlete may attend.
          Moderate Accommodations, may include: breaks as needed during class; begin working
          on missed work/assignments; extended deadlines for assignments; scribe/classmate for
          note taking.

☐ Level 4   Maximum Academic Activities-Full Class Attendance
          Minimal Accommodations; Continue progression back into normal class workload;
          extended time for exams/quizzes/papers (or verbal assessment).

☐ Level 5   Full Academic Activities
          No Accommodations

Figure 4.1a Accommodations for Student-Athlete Recovery from a Concussion

Though these types of services can be critical to student-athlete health, athletic departments are often unable to afford in-house mental health counselors. Likewise, while a few athletic departments employ sport psychology professionals, mental performance/training and mental health are not synonymous. Athletic departments should not ask full-time professionals to serve students both through sport psychology/mental training services and mental health counseling. The needs that make these positions relevant justify the distinct roles and professionals necessary to serve student-athletes.

Signs To Look For After A Concussion
When students return to school after sustaining a concussion, MAC staff should watch for and report to Athletic Medicine:
- Increased problems paying attention or concentrating
- Increased problems remembering or learning new information
- Longer time needed to complete tasks or assignments
- Difficulty organizing tasks or shifting between tasks
- Inappropriate or impulsive behavior during class
- Greater irritability
- Less ability to cope with stress
- More emotional than usual
- Difficulty handling a stimulating school environment (lights, noise, etc.)
- Physical symptoms (headache, dizziness, nausea, visual problems)

In most cases, a concussion will not significantly limit a student's participation in school and usually involves temporary, informal instructional modifications and academic accommodations. Generally, the "Return to Learn" process precedes the "Return to Play" progression. However, a Team Physician may allow monitored exertional activity prior to asymptomatic status. Some cases may take several weeks or months to recover from symptoms of post-concussive syndrome, in which case referral to the DRC for formal accommodations may be indicated.

By completing this document, the sport-specific Athletic Trainer and the Team Physician will help inform decisions about a student-athlete's participation in academic activities. The MAC Staff will then determine the specific need for and level of modification and accommodations, or adjustments, and their readiness to resume various school and physical activities. The recommendations included on this form are based on the current reported signs and symptoms of concussion, the symptom severity, and the medical evaluation of the student-athlete. The Athletic Medicine staff will be re-evaluating the student-athlete daily and will submit updates contemporaneously.

Should you have any questions about the student-athlete's progress or have any observations you wish to pass on to the Athletic Medicine Staff, please don't hesitate to connect.

Sport-Specific Athletic Trainer	Name	Phone number	Email
Director of Athletic Medicine	Jeff Winslow	(612) 616 – 7329	Winslo34@umn.edu

Sincerely,
Name
Title

Cc: MAC Counselor
     JT Bruett
     Team Physician
     Head Coach
     Student-athlete

July 2017

Figure 4.1b Signs to Look for After a Concussion

Mental Health and Well-Being Program Model: Athletes Connected at University of Michigan. At the University of Michigan, a program called Athletes Connected was developed through a collaboration between the School of Public Health, Depression Center, and Athletic Department (University of Michigan, 2017a). The project was started with funding from an NCAA Innovations in Research and Practice Grant to "increase awareness of mental health issues, reduce the stigma of help-seeking, and promote positive coping skills among student-athletes" (University of Michigan, 2017a, para. 1). Athletes Connected has gathered together a team of mental health professionals and athletic staff to run the program. For student-athletes specifically, the program maintains a large amount of resources for them to access. These include restorative yoga sessions, counseling center information, Athletics Counseling Team (ACT) members, campus-wide resources, online resources for Michigan students, and national resources including the National Suicide Prevention Hotline and Crisis Text Line (University of Michigan, 2017c). Information is also provided for mental health and performance, including on body weight and image, peak performance, feeling down, and stress and anxiety. The program also provides skills and strategies for student-athletes including on breathing, cognitive skills, behavioral skills, and other sports psychology resources (University of Michigan, 2017c).

The Athletes Connected team has collected data and is conducting research on different aspects of the program, including videos, team presentations, and drop-in support groups (University of Michigan, 2017b). Information is offered to assist other institutions in implementing similar programs on their own campuses. The program has a variety of videos featuring student-athletes' stories and coping skills related to mental health and well-being topics that anyone can access, including coping with injury, transition into and out of college, and depression and anxiety (University of Michigan, 2017d).

Degree Completion

Student-athletes may leave their institutions before graduating for various reasons. Some exhaust their eligibility to compete, and leave due to other opportunities that arise. Others are drafted to play professional sports. Regardless of the reason, it is a priority for institutions to help former student-athletes finish their degree programs, whether locally or from a distance if possible. While institutions undoubtedly want to help their former students toward graduation for reasons related to their fundamental educational missions, athletic departments have additional incentives to support students toward completion. Student-athletes who complete their degrees may provide an opportunity for athletic departments to adjust graduation metrics that improve their departmental profile (i.e., NCAA Academic Progress Rate (APR), Graduation Success Rate (GSR)). As a result, many athletic departments and institutions work to develop degree-completion programs to support student-athletes in a variety of ways. The following section describes several models that have been shown to be successful.

Rebel Reconnect. The Rebel Reconnect program offers former athletes from the University of Mississippi the chance to finish their degrees with a return to the institution if they meet certain criteria (see Figure 4.2). Rebel Reconnect "assists returning students...with the costs of full or part-time tuition and/or books associated with completing their degree at the University of Mississippi" by offering "employment opportunities in the University of Mississippi Athletic Association" for up to ten hours per week (FedEx Student-Athlete Success Center, 2015, para. 1). Returning students must have received an athletic scholarship before departing the university, and have 30 credits or less to complete with a minimum 2.0 grade point average (GPA). To participate, former student-athletes must be accepted for readmission to the institution, submit the FAFSA, and complete an application to Rebel Reconnect (FedEx Student-Athlete Success Center, 2015).

The Rebel Reconnect program enjoys strong support from the deputy athletic director for sports and administration/SWA and the provost's office. Though the FedEx Student-Athlete Success Center is located in an athletics facility, the center falls under the provost's supervision. Its director explores all channels to identify funding sources, including NCAA post-eligibility scholarships, as well as the Mississippi Complete 2 Compete (C2C) initiative within the state. Leveraging a network of the state's institutions, as well as by offering tuition grants, Mississippi C2C supports students who have left a Mississippi institution more than two years prior in optimizing their path to graduation (MSC2C.org, 2018). Since its implementation, the program has averaged about five graduates per year.

Second Wind. Kansas State University and K-State Athletics offer a program called Second Wind, which helps former K-State athletes complete their degrees if they left school prior to graduating. The program calls on potential participants to "gain one of the most important victories in your life: a college degree" (K-State Athletics, 2018, para. 1). The program offers students two options: an opportunity to complete the degree program residentially, or to finish at a distance through Kansas State University's Global Campus in combination with local institutions.

The residential option supports former student-athletes in returning to campus and provides assistance finding local housing and potential employment opportunities while they work on their degree programs. The opportunity to complete a degree online depends on the degree program availability, so returning students may enroll in a combination of transferable courses from local institutions, online courses through Kansas State University Global Campus, distance courses from other institutions, and potentially test out of certain subjects. Academic counselors work directly with returning students to determine the exact credit hours students need

THE UNIVERSITY OF MISSISSIPPI

FedEx Student-Athlete Success Center
836 All-American Drive
University, MS 38677
(662) 915-7122
Fax: (662) 915-7878
rebelacademics@olemiss.edu

Rebel Reconnect

Rebel Reconnect was established to assist returning student-athletes, who have exhausted their athletic scholarship eligibility, with the costs of full or part-time tuition and/or books associated with completing their degree at the University of Mississippi. Rebel Reconnect provides employment opportunities through the University of Mississippi Athletic Association to allow former scholarship student-athletes the chance to receive financial support to complete their degrees. Participation in the program is approved on a semester-by-semester basis, not to exceed four (4) consecutive semesters. Continued employment in the following semester is based on academic progress and the satisfactory completion of all employment requirements in a given semester.

Eligibility Criteria:

All applicants must meet the following requirements to be eligible to participate in the program:

1. Be accepted for re-admission to the University of Mississippi
2. A completed academic degree plan approved by the specific on-campus academic advisor
3. Must have been a scholarship athlete while attending Ole Miss and not have been dismissed or transferred from the University of Mississippi

Any exceptions to the above must be approved by the Senior Associate Athletic Director of Academic Support, Executive Associate Athletics Director, and the Athletics Director.

A returning student-athlete will be required to work for Athletics in an assigned department for a maximum of 10 hours per week (minimum: 3 hours = 40 hours; 12 hours = 100 hours)

Application Process:

1. Complete and submit a re-admission application online – www.olemiss.edu then click the red Apply button.
2. Review the Rebel Reconnect eligibility criteria. If you do not meet the eligibility criteria then your request for athletic assistance will be reviewed by the Rebel Reconnect committee.
3. Meet with Executive Associate Athletic Director (Lynnette Johnson) to discuss financial assistance and employment agreement. It is your responsibility to schedule a meeting with the Executive Associate Athletic Director (lys@olemiss.edu; 662-915-7303).
4. Schedule an appointment with your on-campus college advisor to discuss graduation plans and your schedule for the upcoming semester.
5. Check and clear any holds that may be on your account by logging on to your (my.olemiss.edu) and, in the main tab, first column, click "Check Holds."
6. Register for classes with Academic Counselor Jon Nance (jnance@olemiss.edu; 662-915-7278).

www.olemisssports.com/academics

Figure 4.2 Rebel Reconnect Program

to graduate, along with a timeline toward graduation based on a schedule they work out together.

Diversity, Equity, and Inclusion

Institutions are now focusing efforts on targeted programming for student-athletes based on their backgrounds and identities. There are emerging student-athlete programming groups for international students, minority students, female students, LGBTQ students, first-generation students, and others within student-athlete services. Colorado State University has a senior athletic staff member focused solely on diversity and inclusion. The University of Illinois and Kansas State University, for example, have formed diversity and inclusion committees within the athletic department that bring together athletics professionals and coaches from different units to innovate for not only their student-athletes, but their departmental culture as well (Fighting Illini, n.d.; K-State Athletics, 2017).

Athletic departments should certainly encourage student-athletes to get involved in organizations and reach out to resource offices on campus, as many campuses offer International Student Centers, Multicultural Centers, Women's Centers, LGBTQ centers and clubs, and even offices serving first-generation students. However, given the time demands of student-athletes, they may not be able to access these spaces of support during regular daytime hours. Student-athletes who are involved in diversity and inclusion efforts through athletic departments can also show more publicly their support for other students and community members who struggle with their identity and fitting in on campus.

International Travel and Student-Athlete Study Abroad Experience

Institutions are also seeking to expose their student-athletes to global experiences, offering travel outside of the United States for community service-oriented programs in a format similar to Alternative Spring Break. These opportunities are not limited to Division I institutions. While study abroad is becoming more common among general students in higher education systems in the United States today, student-athletes still struggle to participate in this form of high-impact practice (Wright & Larsen, 2014). However, those who have studied abroad as student-athletes describe clear positive impacts. First, among the multiple benefits of studying abroad, the most appealing to student-athletes is that it can help develop relationships and perspective. Not only are student-athletes able to enhance their sense of personal identity as they visit places that stretch their problem-solving abilities, they are able to form relationships with their travel companions who are experiencing common challenges (Wright & Larsen, 2012). In turn, the shared experience during study abroad can enhance student-athletes' ability to communicate and live with one another. Therefore, there is an important effect on who and where a student may stay and live that could play a huge role in their experience (Wright & Larsen, 2012).

Cultural Intelligence and Student-Athlete Study Abroad. Next, student-athletes can significantly enhance their sense of cultural knowledge and competence as they are immersed in foreign cultures (Black & Duhon, 2006). Research by Black and Duhon (2006) found that students who took part in the British Studies programs enhanced their cross-cultural tolerance and empathy, self-confidence, and independence. They also determined that the students became more culturally aware from this opportunity to study abroad in the sense of how to greet, speak and collaborate with non-native English speakers. Pre- and post-test surveys given to student-athletes who completed the British Studies program demonstrated clear, positive impacts on self-awareness and knowledge of cultures and society (Black & Duhon, 2006).

Influence of Study Abroad Experience on Identity Development. Next, while student-athletes have limited ability to study abroad, the literature suggests study abroad provides many benefits to college-age students with respect to identity development. More specifically, research shows that studying abroad also assists in students' ability to understand moral and ethical issues, communication skills, academic performance, and overall satisfaction (McLeod & Wainwright, 2009). Studying abroad and global engagement by students has a positive effect on the outcome of the students, especially academically (Luo & Jamieson-Drake, 2015). Further, McLeod and Wainwright (2009) found that successful experiences often led to feelings of increased self-confidence. This research demonstrated that once the students adjust to their situation while studying abroad, they obtained increased self-esteem, realized they were capable of doing more than what they thought they could, and developed a change in self-perception. In addition, as they were forced outside of their comfort zone, they were able to experience many new ideas and situations (McLeod & Wainwright, 2009). In turn, student-athletes described intense personal growth from these experiences. In addition, Wright and Larsen (2012) posited that students who have participated in the studying abroad program have been more civically engaged and in tune with their cultural surroundings. The students return with greater global awareness, are more involved civically, and are more willing to volunteer. Even throughout the participants' lives they continue to see this as one of the most important and fun experiences they have encountered (Wright & Larsen, 2012).

Influence of Study Abroad Experience on Career Development. Next, student-athletes can experience specific benefits related to career development by partaking in study abroad experiences. In fact, Wright and Larsen (2012) commented that many students use studying abroad as a stepping stone to finding an international job. Research conducted from several universities shows that 72.7% of students believe that an employer would find a study abroad experience beneficial for employment and 62.5% of students believe that studying abroad will help them get a job upon graduation (Albers-Miller, Prenshaw, & Straughan, 1999). This experience also gives the students an opportunity to obtain work experience through internships they are given at the school they attend, as well as the opportunity to master a foreign language to excel themselves in future careers (Sanchez, Fornerino, & Zhang, 2006). Research on students studying abroad also demonstrates that those who see this opportunity as a valuable life and career experience have formed positive ideas about studying abroad again in the future (Wang, Gault, Christ, & Diggin, 2016). In turn, studying abroad can enhance career connections and potential internship opportunities for student-athletes.

Barriers to Student-Athlete Study Abroad. Although there are many benefits to studying abroad, there are also challenges students face in the process. General to all study abroad students, research shows that credit transfer can be an issue for those who want to study abroad, as well as faculty support and the cost (Booker, 2001; Clemens, 2003; Hembroff & Rusz, 1993; Lozano, 2008). While research demonstrates specific benefits can be attributed to identity and career development, many barriers still exist with respect to incorporating student-athletes in study abroad experiences. A survey conducted by Symonds (2009) illustrated student-athletes' negative feelings in regards to communication with academics staff, time commitments, and overall satisfaction with their educational experience compared to their non-student-athlete peers. Student-athletes and all college students want to engage in global experiences but do not believe they are able to travel while participating in collegiate athletics or student activities, and stay on track for graduation. Overall, student-athlete study abroad, if offered in an intentional manner, can provide academic and career developmental benefits to student-athletes in terms of high-impact practices (Symonds, 2009).

Increasing Student-Athlete Participation in Study Abroad. Looking at past opportunities developed throughout American institutions can help to contextualize the need for offering study abroad opportunities intentionally for student-athletes. First, to allow more student-athletes to study abroad, the University of Richmond implemented a study abroad program during the summer. By partnering with a university in Spain, the

University of Richmond is able to send up to 30 student-athletes abroad every year (McCarthy, 2016). Macalester College is another example of an NCAA Division III institution that promotes study abroad opportunities for student-athletes. At Macalester College, student-athletes study abroad at the same 60% rate of their non-athlete counterparts. Coaches and administrators speak to their experiences of student-athletes thriving upon graduation and having a heightened sense of a globalized society. The Macalester soccer coach stated that athletes return more sensitive to the world beyond their friends and family and seem more mature (I. Baker, personal communication, January 18, 2010). Through these different experiences and evidence provided, it is shown that, overall, the effect of studying abroad is positive and can assist students in personal and professional growth.

Overall, the literature discussed multiple potential benefits for student-athletes and the intentional incorporation of opportunities in American higher education systems in which student-athletes can participate. Case studies demonstrated how student-athletes thrive upon graduation as they have a heightened sense of cultural competency. Student-athletes are also able to develop strong relationships with students in their study abroad cohort and within the countries to which they travel. In turn, this high-impact practice can provide student-athletes with great personal and professional development benefits academically, socially, and culturally.

Transition Programs

Transition to College. Increasingly, athletic departments have begun to offer transition programs to new student-athletes that go above and beyond the traditional brief orientation. One type of these is known as a "summer bridge" or "bridge" program. Such programs have been common for targeted student populations for some time, but have recently grown more common for student-athletes. Incoming student-athletes (primarily freshmen but sometimes transfers) who receive athletic scholarships often need substantial assistance transitioning to college and the campus environment. Many will begin athletic competitions almost immediately at the start of their first full semester, so the program helps students set realistic expectations about the academic rigor of the institution, helps to identify and locate resources on campus, and meet other students who are experiencing the same transition.

How these programs achieve these goals in practice is varied, but will often bring students to campus during the summer, or a few weeks prior to the start of classes. They will often move into and begin living in residence halls prior to the general student population. The additional time on campus without all of the pressures and responsibilities of the semester, in conjunction with support and resources from advisors and counselors, helps to ease students into college life.

Another type of transition program is the First-Year Experience course or seminar. Many institutions are able to offer a version of this course or seminar tailored toward the student-athlete experience. These courses introduce students to campus resources, time management and organization skills, and other basic life skills for freshmen to develop as new college students. These classes often bring in campus resource experts as guest speakers, so students have an opportunity to meet campus administrators and ask questions in a more intimate setting.

Mamerow and Navarro (2014) proposed two different models of learning communities to serve student-athletes transitioning to college and to aid in their psychosocial development. These two models include a full integration of the student-athletes with the rest of the study population in learning communities, and an exclusive learning community for athletes with linked courses that may benefit student-athlete transition and development. The second model may promote additional beneficial effects related to what is known as "academic clustering" (Mamerow & Navarro, 2014; Pinkerton, Hinz, & Barrow, 1989).

Transition out of College. The NCAA (n.d.-a) offers a resource for student-athletes transitioning out of sport called After the Game: The Former Student-Athlete Experience. After the Game is a coordinated effort providing content and opportunities for different aspects of holistic development. According to the NCAA (n.d.-a), there are four million former NCAA athletes from 1,100 institutions, and the resource "supports [their] lifelong connection to college sports" (para. 1). There is a career center with college athletics-related job postings, a study of former student-athletes regarding life outcomes of former athletes with results posted, an article called "When the Playing Days End," networking events in cities around the United States specifically for former NCAA athletes, and other tips and articles about career development, nutrition, and other topics. The site also shares stories of successful former athletes in various fields, a LinkedIn community, a hashtag, and a place for former athletes to share their stories (NCAA, n.d.-a).

Clemson University Athletics offers transition workshops for seniors who are preparing for life after sport (Lanham, 2019). The student-athletes learn about challenges with athletic identity as they prepare to end their playing days. This workshop is coupled with a resume workshop and a networking event. Clemson's football program hired a professional to specifically organize activities to help its players consider life after sport should professional goals not come to fruition (Hale, 2017).

At the University of California, Berkeley, the football program specifically brings back former student-athletes who are successful in their career fields to network with football student-athletes (Hale, 2017). Institutions have considered offering courses for credit to help student-athletes prepare for their transition out of sport, but the investment has been more in transition courses for incoming student-athletes, who are new to college or the institution. However, offering transition and networking workshops, requiring meetings for seniors with student-athlete services staff, and connecting to other campus resources are potential places to start.

SENSE OF PLACE: FACILITIES FOR ATHLETE SUPPORT

Though not every institution can afford its own student-athlete support facility or space within an athletic facility, the designation of a physical space where athletes can develop a "sense of place" and physically go to for support is becoming more common on many campuses. This is especially true for Division I FBS institutions, where observers have noted a recent facilities arms race (Wolverton, 2008). The facilities (at institutions that can afford them) can make a strong impression on prospective student-athletes during the recruiting process (Bernhard & Bell, 2015). These facilities, however, also serve as a one-stop shop for many of the support services for the student-athlete population. In many cases, they make small but important accommodations such as offering tutoring at the hours when student-athletes are available. Likewise, the training table (where meals are served) might be located with the Academic Center. Further, study rooms, computer labs, and writing support might be offered in these facilities.

There is no prescribed size, budget, location, or slate of offerings for these facilities dictated by college sport governing bodies (Bernhard & Bell, 2015). Several researchers (e.g., Adler & Adler, 1985 Bernhard & Bell, 2015; Pinkerton et al., 1989) have cautioned that these facilities can play a significant (and potentially negative) role in shaping the college experience, in part by isolating student-athletes from the rest of the student body. Some institutions, like the Ohio State University, have chosen to place their athletic facilities in shared spaces inside general academic buildings that are available to all students (Wolverton, 2008). It has become increasingly common, however, to see unusually lavish amenities not typically expected for or by college students, such as napping pods and barber shops, to show up in the latest facilities just for athletes. While these spaces can contribute to isolation, one advantage of designing these spaces especially for student-athletes is that they are typically located near where athletes spend most of their time, such as training and practice facilities. Locating everything in one place can be helpful when students must move between tightly scheduled appointments/commitments (e.g., training room, weight room, practice field). It can be even more beneficial if the athletics facilities are located close to campus buildings and classrooms.

SUMMARY

There are a wide variety of programs and resources for student-athletes at different levels. For two-year institutions, a transfer expert with knowledge of all governing bodies' academic regulations for athletes is a best practice. Institutions with fewer resources may have to get creative in offering support to student-athletes, and make sure their students take advantage of resources available on campus. At institutions with more resources, programs and staff tend to be more specialized. Some athletic departments can offer professionals dedicated to leadership or career development. It is important for student-athlete support services to collaborate with institutional departments outside of athletics to ultimately provide the best college experience for student-athletes, as with the example of the University of Minnesota's Return to Learn policy development. Assessment and data-driven practices are paramount in higher education today to demonstrate student learning and successful outcomes for investment in specific programming.

In Chapter 5, specific examples of model programs at the University of Nebraska, WCU, and UW-Whitewater demonstrate best practices for student-athlete support in Division I, Division II, and Division III respectively.

REFERENCES

Adler, P., & Adler, P. (1985). From idealism to pragmatic detachment: The academic performance of college athletes. *Sociology of Education*, 58(4), 241–250. doi:10.2307/2112226

Albers-Miller, N. D., Prenshaw, P. J., & Straughan, R. D. (1999). Student perceptions of study abroad programs: A survey of US colleges and universities. *Marketing Education Review*, 9(1), 29–36. doi:10.1080/10528008.1999.11488657

Bernhard, L. M., & Bell, L. F. (2015). Location, location, location. In E. Comeaux (Ed.), *Making the connection: Data-informed practices in academic support centers for college athletes* (pp. 125–141). Charlotte, NC: Information Age Publishing.

Black, T., & Duhon, D. (2006). Assessing the impact of business study abroad programs on cultural awareness and personal development. *Journal of Education for Business*, 81(3), 140–144.

Booker, R. W. (2001). *Differences between applicants and non-applicants relevant to the decision to apply to study abroad* (Unpublished doctoral dissertation). University of Missouri, Columbia, MO.

Broughton, E., & Neyer, M. (2001). Advising and counseling student athletes: New Directions for Student Services, *93*, 47–53. https://doi.org/10.1002/ss.4

Chickering, A. W., & Reisser, L. (1993). *Education and Identity*. San Francisco, CA: Jossey-Bass.

Clemens, C. R. (2003). *A descriptive study of demographic characteristics and perceptions of cross-cultural effectiveness of diverse students at Ohio University in relation to study abroad* (Unpublished doctoral dissertation). Ohio University, Athens, OH.

Comeaux, E. (2015). Organizational learning in athletic departments. In E. Comeaux (Ed.), *Making the connection: Data-informed practices in academic support centers for college athletes* (pp. 1–16). Charlotte, NC: Information Age Publishing.

Cooper, J. N. (2015). Strategies for athlete success at historically black colleges and universities. In E. Comeaux (Ed.), *Making the connection: Data-informed practices in academic support centers for college athletes* (pp. 63–77). Charlotte, NC: Information Age Publishing.

Dweck, C. S. (2006). *Mindset: The New Psychology of Success*. New York: Random House.

Farrey, T. (2009, December 12). Seminoles helped by "learning disabled" diagnoses. Retrieved from www.espn.com/espn/otl/news/story?id=4737281

FedEx Student-Athlete Success Center. (2015). *Rebel Reconnect Criteria*. Oxford, MS: The University of Mississippi.

Fighting Illini. (n.d.). Diversity & inclusion. Retrieved from https://fightingillini.com/sports/2017/8/7/diversity-and-inclusion.aspx

Grasgreen, A. (2012, May 9). NCAA academic rules frustrate advisers to athletes. Retrieved from www.insidehighered.com/news/2012/05/09/ncaa-academic-rules-frustrate-advisers-athletes

Grossman, R. (2008, November 28). $6 million center tutors jocks only. *Chicago Tribune*. Retrieved from http://articles.chicagotribune.com/2008-11 28/news/0811270570_1_tutoring-athletes-dumb-jock

Hale, D. M. (2017, July 3). Clemson, Cal leading the way in career training. Retrieved from www.espn.com/college-football/story/_/id/19758226/clemson-tigers-cal-bears-robust-development-programs-preparing-players-life-football

Hembroff, L. A., & Rusz, D. L. (1993). *Minorities and Overseas Studies Programs: Correlates of Differential Participation*. New York, NY: Council on International Educational Exchange.

Hirt, J. B., Amelink, C. T., McFeeters, B. B., & Strayhorn, T. L. (2008). A system of othermothering: Student affairs administrators' perceptions of relationships with students at historically black colleges. *Journal of Student Affairs Research and Practice, 45*(2), 382–408.

K-State Athletics. (2017). *Diversity & inclusion programs.* Retrieved from www.kstatesports.com/sports/2017/9/28/diversity-inclusion-programs.aspx

K-State Athletics. (2018). *Second wind.* Retrieved from www.kstatesports.com/sports/2015/6/17/_131476205148315400.aspx

Lanham, C. (2019). *Developing tigers: Transition workshop.* Retrieved from https://clemsontigers.com/developing-tigers-transition-workshop/

Leach, K. C. (2015, October 16). *NCAA, N4A to partner on life skills professional development.* Retrieved from www.ncaa.org/about/resources/media-center/news/ncaa-n4a-partner-life-skills-professional-development

Lozano, J. E. (2008). *Exploring students' decisions regarding studying abroad: A study of private university students in south Texas* (Doctoral dissertation). Retrieved from ProQuest Dissertations & Theses (UMI No. 3305622)

Luo, J. & Jamieson-Drake, D. (2015). Predictors of study abroad intent, participation, and college outcomes. *Research in Higher Education, 56*(1), 29–56. https://doi.org/10.1007/s11162-014-9338-7

Mamerow, G. P., & Navarro, K. M. (2014). Put me in, coach! Making the academic learning community an option for student-athletes. *Learning Communities Research and Practice, 2*(1), 1–10.

McCarthy, C. (2016). Innovative strategies allow student-athletes to access study abroad, summer internships. *College Athletics and the Law, 13*(6), 12.

McLeod, M., & Wainwright, P. (2009). Researching the study abroad experience. *Journal of Studies in International Education, 13*(1), 66–71. https://doi.org/10.1177/1028315308317219

MSC2C.org. (2018). *What is Complete 2 Compete?* Retrieved from www.msc2c.org/about/

National Collegiate Athletic Association (NCAA). (n.d.-a). *After the game: The former student-athlete experience.* Retrieved from www.ncaa.org/student-athletes/former-student-athlete

National Collegiate Athletic Association (NCAA). (n.d.-b). *Life skills.* Retrieved from www.ncaa.org/about/resources/leadership-development/life-skills

National Collegiate Athletic Association (NCAA). (1999). *NCAA CHAMPS/Life Skills program* [Brochure]. Indianapolis, IN.

National Collegiate Athletic Association (NCAA). (2018). *AASP grants for schools.* Retrieved from www.ncaa.org/about/aasp-grants-schools

Navarro, K. M. (2015). Preparation for life after sport. In E. Comeaux (Ed.), *Making the connection: Data-informed practices in academic support centers for college athletes* (pp. 91–108). Charlotte, NC: Information Age Publishing.

Oregon State Athletics. (2018). *Beyond football – preparing for life.* Retrieved from http://osubeavers.com/sports/2014/7/1/209536391.aspx

Palmer, R., & Gasman, M. (2008). "It takes a village to raise a child": The role of social capital in promoting academic success for African American men at a black college. *Journal of College Student Development, 49*(1), 52–70. https://doi.org/10.1353/csd.2008.0002

Pinkerton, R. S., Hinz, L. D., & Barrow, J. C. (1989). The college student-athlete: Psychological considerations and interventions. *Journal of American College Health, 37*(5), 218–226. https://doi.org/10.1080/07448481.1989.9939063

Raglin, T. (2017, January 23). Marissa Nichols, athletics first director of leadership, career development. *BU Today.* Retrieved from www.bu.edu/today/2018/marissa-nichols-athletics-first-director-of-leadership-career-development/

Sánchez, C. M., Fornerino, M., & Zhang, M. (2006). Motivations and the intent to study abroad among U.S., French, and Chinese students. *Journal of Teaching in International Business, 18*(1), 27–52. doi:10.1300/J066v18n01_03

Symonds, M. L. (2009). Monitoring student engagement for intercollegiate athletics program review. *The International Journal of Educational Management, 23*(2), 161–171. doi:10.1108/09513540910933512

Thamel, P. (2006, November 4). Athletes get new college pitch: Check out our tutoring center. *New York Times.* Retrieved from www.nytimes.com/2006/11/04/sports/ncaafootball/04ncaa.html

University of Arkansas Student-Athlete Development. (2018). *Mission.* Retrieved from www.arkansasrazorbacks.com/student-athlete-development/osas-mission/University of Illinois at Chicago Athletics. (2018). *Staff directory.* Retrieved from http://uicflames.com/staff.aspx

University of Michigan. (2017a). *Athletes connected: About.* Retrieved from https://athletesconnected.umich.edu/about

University of Michigan. (2017b). *Athletes connected: Research.* Retrieved from https://athletesconnected.umich.edu/for-researchers

University of Michigan. (2017c). *Athletes connected: Student-athletes.* Retrieved from https://athletesconnected.umich.edu/for-student-athletes

University of Michigan. (2017d). *Athletes connected: Videos.* Retrieved from https://athletesconnected.umich.edu/videos

University of Minnesota Athletic Medicine. (2017a). *Concussion management plan.* Minneapolis, MN.

University of Minnesota Athletic Medicine. (2017b). *Accommodations for student-athlete recovering from a concussion.* Minneapolis, MN.

Vanderbilt University. (n.d.). *Challenging athletes' minds for personal success.* Retrieved from https://wp0.vanderbilt.edu/champs

Wang, L. C., Gault, J., Christ, P. & Diggin, P. A. (2016). Individual attitudes and social influences on college students' intent to participate in study abroad programs. *Journal of Marketing for Higher Education, 26*(1), 103–128. doi:10.1080/08841241.2016.1146385

Wolverton, B. (2008, September 5). Spending plenty so athletes can make the grade. *Chronicle of Higher Education, 55*(2), A1.

Wolverton, B. (2016, February 28). The hottest hire in athletics? Learning specialists. *Chronicle of Higher Education.* Retrieved from www.chronicle.com/article/The-Hottest-Hire-in-Athletics-/235513

Wright, N., & Larsen, V. (2012). Every brick tells a story: Study abroad as an extraordinary experience. *Marketing Education Review, 22,* 121–142.

Yang, J., Peek-Asa, C., Corlette, J. D., Cheng, G., Foster, D. T., & Albright, J. (2007). Prevalence of and risk factors associated with symptoms of depression in competitive collegiate student athletes. *Clinical Journal of Sport Medicine, 17*(6), 481–487.

Chapter Five

Program Models Across Divisions
Case Studies at Division I, II, and III Institutions

This chapter presents an overview of three program models within each NCAA division. The Division I model showcases the University of Nebraska's comprehensive student-athlete services model, including academic support and student-athlete development programming. The Division II model describes a collaboration across the growing WCU campus to involve various units within academic affairs and student affairs to ensure student-athlete success at an institution offering one of the largest Division II athletic programs. The Division III model navigates the development and implementation of a leadership academy at UW-Whitewater, the first of its kind in this division, to champion holistic student-athlete development and success.

DIVISION I COMPREHENSIVE PROGRAM MODEL: UNIVERSITY OF NEBRASKA

The University of Nebraska provides a model of excellence for student-athlete development and academic success. Many attributes of Nebraska's model make it distinctive in the college athletics landscape, even among NCAA Division I institutions and Power 5 peers. Like other colleges with nationally recognized college sports programs, Nebraska has offered academic support services for student-athletes for decades. Nebraska is unique, however, in the tenure and longevity it has maintained among its leadership and staff, a characteristic that is atypical across an ever-changing college athletics landscape that is known for significant turnover. Stable leadership and staff have contributed to the quality of its initiatives, and the program has garnered numerous accolades and accomplishments, including a nation-leading 333 Division I Academic All-Americans at the time of printing.

History of Nebraska's Student-Athlete Support Services and its Leadership

In the late 1980s, Dennis Leblanc moved from track coach to a new role as an academic counselor at Nebraska. As a coach, he had managed admissions and other administrative processes, so he applied those skills to this new role. At the same time, Keith Zimmer joined the unit as an academic counselor. In the early 1990s, the NCAA officially launched the CHAMPS/Life Skills program. Zimmer attended an NCAA CHAMPS/Life Skills training seminar, and began a decade of dual responsibilities, as both academic counselor and coordinating life skills programming for the entire unit. By 1993, Leblanc was interim director of Nebraska's student-athlete programming, and by that point both he and Zimmer had worked together for many years, and had built a positive and supportive culture in the office.

In 1997, Jo Potuto, the Richard H. Larson Professor of Constitutional Law at Nebraska College of Law, assumed the duties of Nebraska's FAR, a position in which she continues to serve to this day. Her tenure in the position is just one indicator of the strong rapport and positive working and personal relationships that have developed among the leadership. She has extensive leadership experience in conference governance for both the Big 12 and Big Ten, as well as service on numerous NCAA committees. Potuto has also served as president of 1A FARs.

Throughout the time Leblanc and Zimmer have worked in student-athlete support at Nebraska, the department has had six ADs. According to Leblanc, all have been supportive of academics and other student-athlete development efforts. The investment in these areas by the AD is crucial and enables a culture of success for students to thrive. In contrast to Nebraska's example, in some units across the country, academics and life skills/student-athlete development professionals compete for students' time, resulting in friction between these areas. At Nebraska, however, the long-standing relationship between Leblanc and Zimmer has prevented any issues.

Leblanc was promoted to Associate Athletic Director, then to Senior Associate Athletic Director for Academic Programs and Student Services, and in 2015, was named Executive Associate Athletic Director for Academics. As he progressed in his career, Leblanc received the prestigious Lan Hewlett Award from the N4A, which recognizes one outstanding leader and administrator in the field annually.

When the legendary Tom Osborne became AD at Nebraska, he created a life skills unit for Zimmer to manage in 2008 as Senior Associate Athletic Director for Life Skills. Both units specialize in their own areas but have an aligned vision based on the history of the unit leaders' working together. According to Zimmer:

> Longevity of staff leads to trust, respect, comfort level between campus and athletics – we get good cooperation because people know Dennis and I will do the right thing, we never had a hidden agenda – we truly believe in that spirit of collaboration.
> (Zimmer, personal communication, May 4, 2018)

In an era where colleges and universities do not always recognize the relevance and positive contribution athletic departments can make toward institutions' educational missions, Nebraska Athletics is a powerful example of how to develop a strong relationship between institution, administration, faculty, and staff. Zimmer further highlights that in his vision, athletics wants to be a partner with the university, to work collectively and to be transparent.

Facilities and Budget

Both the academic and life skills units are housed in the west side of Memorial Stadium on the University of Nebraska campus. The space has undergone several renovations since its inception, each time expanding spaces to better serve students through improved design. Student-athletes provided input on what space and resources were needed for their success, and that feedback was incorporated into the layout of the space. Up through 2010, the space was 9,500 square feet; by the end of 2010, it had increased to 31,200 square feet. The latest renovation plan for 2018 includes changing the computer lab into a learning commons/study area (removing desktop computers since all student-athletes are now provided laptops), creating additional study rooms, and reorganizing the learning specialists' office areas. The athletic dining hall/training table is located next to the academic and life skills units, requiring athletes to walk past the area between their locker rooms and exercise facilities en route to meals. Coaches and administrators also dine here, where they can see student-athletes studying.

The facility is named the Dick and Peg Herman Family Student Life Complex. The Herman family has provided support for these units for decades. It has six areas: the Hewit Academic Center, the Abbott Life Skills Center, the DJ Sokol Enrichment Center, the Scott Technology Center, the Papik Compliance Center, and the Lewis Training Table (NU Athletic Communications, 2018). What is especially unique about the student-athlete support facility at Nebraska is its location. Though it is in the stadium, the center is only a five- to seven-minute walk from most classes. Not only is it located near food (a critical concern for training athletes), but it is also within a minute's walk of tutoring, a full-time physician, film rooms, and the weights room. This enhances student-athlete engagement and interaction, including interaction among teammates and with administrators, as the spaces include all of the various areas each group must pass through and use each day. Though other institutions may have a bigger overall budget, their facilities may not compare favorably in terms of distance from campus, classes, or other athletic amenities. Institutions have dispatched their academic leadership to visit Nebraska and tour its facilities for ideas.

The operating budget without staff salaries for the academic unit is around $330,000 with an additional technology budget of $125,000. The salaries cover full-time staff, benefits, tutors, and student workers, nearing $1.2 million. In total, the academic budget is just under $1.7 million. In the life skills unit, the operating budget without salaries is approximately $300,000. The unit employs a much smaller staff than the academic unit. The staff are the key to the success of these areas of academics and life skills.

Staff

In college athletics, it is not uncommon to see high turnover in departments as people move around the country for new opportunities. What is unusual about Nebraska is the longevity of tenure among staff, indicating a strong loyalty to the institution and the students it serves. According to Leblanc, "The people that work here make Nebraska unique and different from everybody else...What we do revolves around the people who work here and have their buy-in, be a part of it, and have success with it" (personal communication, May 23, 2018). Currently, the academics staff includes Leblanc and 13 full-time professionals, including three learning specialists. The life skills staff includes Zimmer and four full-time professionals. In the mid-1990s, Leblanc and Zimmer discussed with athletic administration a way to develop up-and-coming professionals while adding staff that were not considered full-time, permanent positions. These discussions led to the launching of the Assistant Academic Counselor (AAC) program, essentially a 2-year, full-time internship experience that immerses talented people with Master's degrees to jump-start their careers in student-athlete services. Depending on the year, there are as many as five AACs working in the academic center. Before the academic and life skills units separated, an AAC might have had split duties for both academics and life skills. Now, life skills can have its own assistant life skills counselor(s). This model has been implemented at many other institutions since Nebraska started it, though it is now more common to see one-year full-time internship positions rather than two-year opportunities.

Performance Evaluations and Standards. At Nebraska, staff set annual goals for their performance. When developing goals, staff keep in mind the athletic department's mission and core values. The academic program also has its own vision, mission, core competencies, and guiding principles that inform staff goals. The academic program vision is to "Provide the most comprehensive, nationally recognized, academic enhancement program in college athletics" (Nebraska Athletics, 2018a, p. 1). The academic program mission is "Through expertise and continuity, we passionately serve student-athletes by fostering transition, retention and graduation" (Nebraska Athletics, 2018a, p. 1). The academic program core competencies include to "enhance recruitment, model integrity, monitor eligibility, recognize achievement and achieve graduation," and its guiding principles are to "serve student-athletes, operate with integrity, communicate and collaborate effectively, function as a team and be passionate" (Nebraska Athletics, 2018a, p. 1). The entire academics unit has a shared goal to achieve a GSR of 90%. When staff have regular one-on-one meetings with Leblanc, their annual goals appear on the agenda so they are consistently in the conversation. Leblanc develops a plan with each staff member to help each person achieve the goals set for the year.

Student-Athlete Development/Life Skills Programs

Zimmer is likewise a recognized leader in the life skills/student-athlete development field. In 1989, Nebraska won the inaugural Life Skills Program of Excellence Award and in 2006, Zimmer was named the CHAMPS/Life Skills Administrator of the Year. He has been focused on this area since the late 1980s, yet did not have his own unit at Nebraska until 2008. Around the country, there has been a trend toward athletic departments separating the academics and student-athlete development areas, including by staff, facilities, and budgets. According to Zimmer, positions like his do not typically have a seat at the highest table (senior athletic staff), but he has a senior position, and believes that, in time, professionals in this area will and should be part of the senior athletic staff. Under his leadership, the unit focuses on student development, leadership, and service. This encompasses community involvement and outreach, career development, personal development, and overall well-being, as well as advising the SAAC.

One of the reasons it is important for a life skills or student-athlete development administrator to be on senior staff is the sheer depth of issues facing student-athletes and athletic department staff (e.g., mental health, social climate, race relations/diversity, sexual assault, violence prevention). These issues require substantial attention and investment by the AD, and the entire department needs to be proactive to minimize the possibility of serious issues arising. A major focus of Zimmer's staff is ongoing training for staff and coaches on topics like communicating with athletes and diversity, equity, and inclusion. Zimmer and his staff work hard to develop and maintain relationships with campus and community partners. He suggested, "Everything we have done has been on that foundation of growing it the right way, integrating with existing resources on campus" (K. Zimmer, personal communication, May 4, 2018). The office often coordinates with the career center, Education Abroad, Graduate Studies, the Women's Center, and the Multicultural Center. As a result, student-athletes are able to interact with campus resource experts who are readily available to other students, and better know who to talk to and where on campus to go if they need support or have questions. The life skills unit has also developed community partnerships with Lincoln Public Schools, local hospitals, and the Lincoln Track Club. Reflecting on these partnerships, Zimmer emphasized:

> We never just create and isolate and do our own thing – people want to feel a connection and a part of this program because this program is special and it means something to a lot of people – they want to be affiliated with it or in many cases help with it so why would you want to turn that help away? Embrace it.
> (Personal communication, May 4, 2018)

One of the newest initiatives developed by the life skills team is a social climate group called N-Volved, which started in January 2018. It required students to apply for 30 spots. The group offers a space for students to have difficult conversations on topics like race relations, gun violence, religion, and gender identity. Its vision is to provide an ongoing outlet for students to engage in deeper conversations about challenging topics, and to participate beyond merely listening to a speaker without an opportunity to offer personal perspective, reflect, or find closure. It is designed to be a caring environment for students to listen and be heard, and participating students partner with LGBTQA groups, the Women's Center, and Multicultural Center, support one another's events and share resources.

Zimmer continues to build impactful partnerships on campus. Currently, he collaborates with the Master of Arts in Business with a specialization in Intercollegiate Athletic Administration through Nebraska's College of

Business, to place graduate students in athletic department internships. He also serves as a sport administrator to several athletic teams.

Post-eligibility Opportunities (PEO) Program

Dennis Leblanc had long been bothered by the lack of opportunities for students who became professional athletes but did not have other work experience. When the NCAA changed its rules allowing institutions to provide student-athletes cost of attendance money in addition to scholarships in 2015, he checked with the compliance office to see if Nebraska could offer scholarships to student-athletes who had graduated and finished competing for Nebraska. His inquiry led to a collaboration across athletic department units to begin exploring ways the department could support former students. Learning Specialist Joann Ross came up with the term "post-eligibility opportunities." A year later, after the idea had been developed sufficiently, a coordinator was hired for the new program with the support of the AD, and joined the life skills unit staff. Since its debut in 2016, it has been recognized in the media and by professional organizations with awards and accolades.

The PEO program's mission statement is to "provide unmatched educational experiences to recent letterwinner graduates, increasing their marketability, personal development and intellectual growth" (NU Athletic Communications, 2017, para. 1). The PEO program:

> provides letterwinner alumni a one-semester scholarship, valued up to $7,500, to apply toward an internship, study abroad experience or graduate school at the University of Nebraska-Lincoln or the University of Nebraska Medical Center. Eligible letterwinner alumni, who fulfill all program requirements, will have up to three years from the time of graduation or exhaustion of eligibility, whichever occurs latest, to participate in this program.
> (NU Athletic Communications, 2017)

The program has specific participation eligibility requirements including that students must: have graduated in or after December 2015; have earned a varsity letter and scholar-athlete ring; have exhausted eligibility; have attended and completed the PEO Success Series Workshops; have received an internship, study abroad, or graduate school (UNL or UNMC) acceptance offer; and have enrolled in PEO-related class credit (NU Athletic Communications, 2017). Since its inception, the PEO program has distributed $850,000 in aid to 121 participants from six continents, 14 countries, and 18 states. It boasts having had its participants in 75 domestic internships, 12 international internships, 15 study abroad trips, 12 enrollments in graduate school, and seven enrollments in medical school. Perhaps the greatest testament to its success, participants have a 98% job placement and retention rate (Nebraska Athletics, 2018b). PEO has an annual budget of approximately $1 million. The program creates opportunities for graduated student-athletes in which many non-athlete students participate during their time in school (such as internships and study abroad) but which do not necessarily fit into the schedules of student-athletes. To further describe the vision behind the program, Zimmer explained:

> Time demands and student-athlete welfare surveys showed students cannot keep up with much except a little community service beyond academics and athletics (no time to plan for my future by doing anything significant) – they want grad school preparation, internship opportunities, study abroad – but sport is year round including summer, so give them help when they are done with athletics and have more time, continue to see this through until we make you better. We can't give them the money when they are an undergraduate student-athlete so why not do the right thing and give them the means to be successful after they exhaust eligibility? Other schools have the money but a lot of it goes to coaches. It takes courage from an AD and vision from the program – coaches love it as a recruiting tool. Ultimately it impacts real people and their future.
> (Personal communication, May 4, 2018)

Despite its short history, the PEO program has proven its impact with its successful placement rate both qualitatively and quantitatively, including students enrolled in graduate and medical programs. It is suggested here that athletic departments might benefit from investing in a program like this for graduates—rather than engaging in typical investment approaches, including numerous other areas that may not directly benefit students (see Figure 5.1a and b).

Awards Banquet

The Herman family, for whom the student life complex is named, also made the celebration of achievement not only possible but central to the culture at Nebraska by establishing an endowed fund in 1989 to support an annual academic banquet. This banquet honors athletes who achieve at least a 3.00 calendar year or cumulative GPA with medallions (bronze for GPA 3.00–3.49, silver for 3.50–3.749, gold for 3.750–4.00). The banquet

POST-ELIGIBILITY
OPPORTUNITIES PROGRAM
SETTING THE STANDARD FOR LIFE BEYOND ATHLETICS

- **LETTER** in a varsity sport
- **GRADUATE** December 2015 or after
- **EXHAUST** eligibility
- **EARN** Scholar-Athlete Ring

ATTEND & COMPLETE PEO Success Series Workshops

RESEARCH & APPLY FOR AN . . .

| INTERNSHIP | STUDY ABROAD PROGRAM | GRADUATE SCHOOL (UNL / UNMC) |

Get accepted and enroll in PEO-related class credit to receive up to a **$7,500 SCHOLARSHIP** for an internship, study abroad experience or graduate school

IMPACT

$850,000 PEO AID DISTRIBUTED | 121 PARTICIPANTS

6 CONTINENTS | 14 COUNTRIES | 18 STATES

| 75 | 12 | 15 | 12 | 7 |
| DOMESTIC INTERNSHIPS | INTERNATIONAL INTERNSHIPS | STUDY ABROAD | GRADUATE SCHOOL | MEDICAL SCHOOL |

98% JOB PLACEMENT RATE

2017 NACE CHEVRON AWARD

1 *USA TODAY*, 1 *ATHLETIC MANAGEMENT MAGAZINE* & 1 *LandOfTen.com* FEATURE

CAMPUS PARTNERS

Figure 5.1a Post-eligibility Opportunities Program

INTERNSHIP EVALUATION

Evaluation Area (Based On 5-Point Scale)	Score
Learned information, skills or techniques not learned in class	4.57
Gained career, professional knowledge	4.53
Gained greater self-confidence	4.54
Improved understanding of strengths/weaknesses	4.48
Met individuals who contributed to professional growth	4.75
Overall experience rating from intern	4.58
Overall performance rating from supervisor	4.57

PARTICIPATE IN PEO

"
Participating in the PEO program is a no-brainer. The option for each student-athlete to tailor their PEO experience to their own personal post-graduate goals is proof Nebraska Athletics cares deeply about the continued development of each and every Husker student-athlete well above and beyond their athletic performance. Whether an internship, study abroad experience, or graduate school, PEO helps relieve or completely reduce the financial strains of your transition out of college.

Melanie Crawford | Bowling | 2017 PEO Internship Participant

PARTICIPANT TESTIMONIALS

Dawna Tyson, Nebraska Softball Alum
Pathfinder Support Services Family Support Worker (Lincoln, Neb.)

"PEO allowed me to submerge myself without worrying about finances. I enhanced my understanding of community resources for parents/families that battle addictions/poverty and showed parents they could do things they thought impossible to help their children and family. I discovered my passion for the field and want to go back to school to get a degree in social work."

Jake Sueflohn, Nebraska Wrestling Alum
Purdue Athletics Volunteer Wrestling Coach (West Lafayette, Ind.)

"PEO allowed me to do something few others get to do - work as a volunteer coach at a Big Ten program and experience what it's like to have the job I've always wanted. I gained knowledge on being a college coach and areas I can improve, greater awareness of behind-the-scenes happenings, and confidence in my abilities to excel in future college coaching opportunities."

Tess Merrill, Nebraska Track & Field Alum
Tower-London Research Analyst Intern (London, England)

"While abroad, I experienced a new culture and set of norms. I saw first-hand the impact Brexit had on employees and daily business activities and gained experience with online financial programs, identifying relevant data to use when creating reports. This once-in-a-lifetime experience greatly increased my confidence and has served as a strong stepping stone in my career."

Chongo Kondolo, Nebraska Football Alum
AmeriCorps Youth on the Move Internship (Lincoln, Neb.)

"If not for PEO, I would have had to work a job that wasn't in my career interest area because that would have been the only way for me to pay my bills. With PEO, I interned as a youth mentor with AmeriCorps' Youth on the Move program, gained experience in the career field I wanted to enter, and secured a full-time position in family services working with area youth."

Figure 5.1b Post-eligibility Opportunities Program (continued)

is a cooperative event supported by both the academics and life skills units. The budget for the event is $130,000, and up to 1,400 people attend annually. At the very first banquet in 1991, 162 medallions were awarded, and most recently, 315 were given to deserving students.

Because of the event's scale, it is now a combination of recognition for academics, athletics, and service, and the ceremony recognizes students for a variety of accomplishments in a unique setting. It is designed to mimic major awards ceremonies like the ESPY Awards, with an emcee and full orchestra. Life skills staff work on the creative side and production, while academics staff focus on the behind-the-scenes work, catering, invitations/RSVPs, and logistics. Through the Herman family's generous gift, Nebraska is able to celebrate all of its student-athletes' achievements on a grand scale.

Culture, Brand, and Policies

At the University of Nebraska, across the Big Ten Conference, and nationally, Nebraska's student-athlete services, day in and day out, bring expression to the brand of Academic Excellence. When recruits visit campus, rather than thinking "Why Nebraska?" staff want prospective students and their families to think "Why not?" Indeed, after touring the facilities and learning about the resources and dedicated staff, few recruits would disagree that Nebraska is a major contender for consideration, for reasons far beyond athletic opportunities. In 2008, the academic unit developed a strategic plan to improve graduation rates, and since 2010, they have improved by 16%. With support from athletic staff, students are achieving the highest-ever NCAA academic metrics in the history of the program, specifically with respect to APR and GSR. Since development of the strategic plan, coaches have targeted an APR standard of at least 950.

In another example of Nebraska Athletic's tradition of collaboration across units, professionals from academics, athletic certification (initial eligibility and continuing eligibility/progress-toward-degree), staff in the registrar's office, and key staff in the compliance office came together to form what became known as Nebraska's Academics Eligibility Compliance (AEC) group. Working together, the team engages in weekly communication while reviewing the needs of incoming students and initial eligibility. Their discussions frequently focus on changes to NCAA bylaws that may impact their work, as well as ways to improve students' experiences. Coaches with concerns about policies or individual athletes are invited to meetings to discuss them, and the group works together in a collaborative manner to address issues that arise. Similarly, a team of professionals from these units evaluates the transcripts of recruited athletes to ensure that more than one person has the opportunity to evaluate the strengths, weakness, and needs of potential members of the Nebraska family.

Leblanc stressed that he "works in the trenches," by meeting directly with coaches to be the first point of contact and communication before his staff get involved, and to provide guidance whenever a disagreement may arise (personal communication, May 23, 2018). Moreover, the unit has developed policies over time to guide athletic staff with respect to who can communicate with other campus offices (e.g., admissions, financial aid, and academic departments). Such polices were instituted, not to stifle communication, but to ensure that information reaches the correct parties (i.e., those with the power and responsibility to address specific issues). The policies specify, for example, which designated academic and compliance staff can communicate with specific campus offices. Leblanc and his two associate directors begin by communicating orally with faculty. This, in turn, is followed up with written documentation of any matters discussed. Other academics staff are required to use e-mail to communicate with faculty regarding students' academic progress. When travel for competition requires student-athletes' exams to be proctored at another institution, policies dictate that a faculty member at the hosting institution proctor the exam, rather than a staff member or other campus employee. Likewise, when athletes traveling to Nebraska for a competition must sit for an academic examination, a member of the academics staff will contact a Nebraska faculty member to proctor the visiting athlete's exam.

Many of the unit's services have expanded in recent years; more than half of incoming student-athletes now participate in the summer bridge program. Staff also oversee a new program that provides each student-athlete with a laptop upon arrival that must be returned upon graduation. The unit has been expanded to include three full-time learning specialists who support students with additional academic resources. Leblanc monitors student-athletes who exhaust eligibility but still have credits remaining before graduation. He works closely with compliance to explore funding possibilities that may help them graduate. His constant advocacy in this area has helped to identify resources which now can amount to a full scholarship to help expired eligibility athletes complete a degree. In addition, as mentioned previously, facilities are under constant review for potential updates that can better serve student-athletes.

Overall, assessment plays a substantial role in the culture of athletics at Nebraska. Leblanc collects metrics, not just for the NCAA's APR and GSR reporting, but to inform various aspects of the overall program. In addition to PEO outcome metrics, Zimmer examines the impact of community outreach by examining the number of sponsored service projects, number of community members engaged, and the number of students named to the

Tom Osborne Citizenship Team (athletes who complete six or more service projects in a year). The SAAC conducts a survey of the athlete population, then meets with the AD to share feedback directly. Each team participates in an end-of-the-year evaluation of its head coach, as well as the team overall. Results are reported to the team's sport administrator. All seniors complete exit interviews with athletic administrators to learn more about their experiences and recommendations about how Nebraska can improve. All of these data sources are shared, not just within the athletic department but also with its stakeholders through the athletic department's annual report. The report's first ten pages are dedicated to sharing the successes of academic and life skills programs, before discussion of athletic-related successes. All of the unique aspects of Nebraska's comprehensive student-athlete support program, including its loyal staff, longevity in leadership, focus on collaboration, and investment in student-athlete development, make it a model program in college athletics today.

DIVISION II COLLABORATIVE MODEL: WEST CHESTER UNIVERSITY

West Chester University (WCU) in Pennsylvania has one of the largest Division II athletics programs in the NCAA, with approximately 545 student-athletes on 24 teams (Hodes, James, Martin & Milliner, 2015). NCAA Division II institutions have academic benchmarks their student-athletes must meet to be eligible for competition. According to Hodes et al. (2015), "WCU has grown from a local state school to a much more selective public institution" (p. 50). An increase in applications has decreased the acceptance rate, increased the number of out-of-state students to 13%, and increased the amount of under-represented minority students to 19% in 2014 (Hodes et al., 2015). In 2014, the rapid growth led to a student population of almost 13,000 undergraduates and over 2,000 graduate students (Hodes et al., 2015).

WCU has emphasized the importance of maintaining or increasing its retention rate as well as is its four- and six-year graduate rates. The first-to second-year retention rate in 2013–2014 was 87.9%, and the six-year graduation rate for students entering in fall 2008 was 66.9% (Hodes et al., 2015). Yet WCU has faced some challenges that impact its students' success. The first is an increase in the number of students conditionally admitted through the "Summer Bridge Academic Development Program (ADP)" or as special admission students who are allowed to enroll only in 12 credits in the first semester (Hodes et al., 2015, pp. 51–52). Of those conditionally admitted students, 178 of the 368 (48%) first-year student-athletes were part of that group, which is a large number of the incoming athlete population (Hodes et al., 2015). Another major challenge WCU has faced is common among public institutions: "As a mid-sized public, state-system institution, WCU has faced extreme budgetary issues over the past decade" (Hodes et al., 2015, p. 52). The third challenge was that the athletic department only had three staff members who run every aspect of operations, "including but not limited to event management, fundraising, NCAA compliance, facilities management, operational and scholarship budget oversight, personnel, equipment management, student-athlete support and academic services" (Hodes et al., 2015, p. 53). This is an enormous amount of labor for three people to manage at any institution.

These challenges have led university leadership to encourage collaboration across campus to offer programs with high-impact practices that help students be academically successful (Hodes et al., 2015). Different units on campus were already doing various activities and offering support for student-athletes, but not working together. For example, the Learning Assistance and Resource Center (LARC), which "houses tutoring, Supplemental Instruction, and the Early Alert programs," offered academic support for athletes on academic probation or who received Early Alerts from faculty, but the staff were overwhelmed (Hodes et al., 2015, p. 55). The Department of Health, an academic unit, offered a course HEA 208: Leadership/Life Skills for Student-Athletes, which targeted first- and second-year student-athletes. Hodes et al. (2015) described:

> The course is designed to provide student-athletes with basic life skills and leadership training to become successful students at WCU. Contents of the course include, but are not limited to, time management, study skills/habits, academic planning, campus resources, stress management, healthy lifestyle practices (including nutrition, alcohol use, tobacco use and drug abuse), goal-setting, decision-making, conflict resolution, team building and community advocacy.
>
> (p. 53)

This is a great resource for student-athletes that counted as elective credit. Yet between the Department of Health, the athletic department, and the LARC, there was no coordination of efforts. The athletic department also hired academic mentors to work with athletes in the LARC, but there were only three who were meeting with a large number of students. WCU then aimed to "create a unique, collaborative model for supporting our student-athletes academically, socially, and personally" (Hodes et al., 2015, pp. 47–48).

Campus Collaborations

WCU's provost appointed a faculty academic coordinator "to monitor student-athletes' academic progress," supervise mentors, liaise with offices including the LARC and the Office of Services for Students with Disabilities, and "[maintain] a comprehensive database of student use and support and tutorial services and [prepare] reports accordingly" (Hodes et al., 2015, p. 53). This coordinator's work took pressure off of the athletic department staff who were doing these types of activities on top of all other tasks. The next collaborative idea was to hire mentors for student-athletes that had experience working with athletes or as athletes themselves. WCU has a CACREP-accredited graduate program in Higher Education Counseling/Student Affairs which requires its students to complete experience-related hours. The LARC hired and supervised ten to 14 graduate students from this program each semester to serve as academic mentors for student-athletes who were considered to be at risk or deemed academically ineligible (Hodes et al., 2015). The LARC also provided study space, study hall monitors, and tutors for courses that athletes struggled in (e.g., math, chemistry) (Hodes et al., 2015).

Students who were considered at risk or deemed ineligible participated in the athletic mentoring program. Hodes et al. (2015) explained:

> In Fall 2014, 63 students were enrolled in the athletic mentoring program and were required to attend four to six hours a week of study hall. Seventeen students were added mid-semester to the program. For the 90 students enrolled in the program, the average number of hours attended over the semester was two per week and the average number of hours completed for the semester was a total of 32 hours per student. The Athletic Study Hall had a total of 2,334 contact hours for the Fall 2014 semester. A total of 46 students completed between 28–70 hours during the fourteen-week study hall program.
>
> (p. 56)

Documenting student-athlete use of space, study hours, mentoring, and tutoring enabled WCU to justify its collaboration across units. The major takeaway from all of these efforts was "remember to be data driven" (Hodes et al., 2015, p. 56).

WCU required all student-athletes in the at-risk and ineligible status to "attend all academic success meetings, obtain a tutor, and attend study hall" (Hodes et al., 2015, p. 54). The faculty academic coordinator also met weekly with mentors to review any issues with specific student-athletes. Given the financial challenges facing WCU as a public institution, this program has continued successfully with "very little budgetary support" (Hodes et al., 2015, p. 56). WCU also continues to offer the Leadership and Life Skills for Student-Athletes course as an elective option for underclassmen student-athletes. According to Hodes et al. (2015):

> The key to the success at WCU was three-fold: 1. keeping student-athlete success at the forefront of the conversation, 2. finding possible and mutually beneficial solutions to each area involved, and 3. breaking down silos so as to not duplicate services.
>
> (p. 56)

The collaboration truly reached across the campus, involving the provost, faculty, LARC, Office of Services for Students with Disabilities, the Department of Health, the athletic department, the graduate program in Higher Education Counseling/Student Affairs, and students who worked as tutors, mentors, and study hall monitors. The efforts connect directly to WCU's desire to maintain and increase retention and graduate rates, as almost half of incoming student-athletes are conditionally admitted and the institution is becoming more selective. This collaborative model at the Division II level is exemplary in focusing on student-athlete success given the context of a growing, public institution with a large athletic program and academic benchmarks to reach.

DIVISION III CASE STUDY: UW-WHITEWATER WARHAWK LEADERSHIP ACADEMY

Program Overview

The Warhawk Leadership Academy (WLA) was the first of its kind in Division III, designed to support holistic student-athlete development, and to organize a variety of support programs into a coherent curriculum. Planning for the academy began in the fall of 2013, when Dr. Kristina Navarro and Director of Athletics Amy Edmonds first put plans in motion to develop, implement, and assess the WLA at UW-Whitewater. Drawing on contemporary research in intercollegiate athletics, the expertise of the founding directors, the needs of the UW-Whitewater athletics community, and input from stakeholders, the WLA was established with the primary goal of developing and delivering a comprehensive model NCAA Division III curriculum that would prepare student-athletes for success in athletics, academics, and life.

The WLA spans the length of a student-athlete's four years in school at UW-Whitewater. The freshman year focuses on personal enhancement, social responsibility, career development, and leadership by having participants (known as Rising Warhawks) enroll in two one-credit courses—one in fall, one in spring—that very intentionally connect students with a wide range of campus resources and support, much of which is provided through partnership with other campus units. During the sophomore year, the curricular emphasis shifts to Campus and Community Outreach and Civic Leadership, and participants are provided opportunities (known as Warhawk Outreach) to practice their growing skills in the community. As juniors, the student-athletes (now called Veteran Warhawks) focus on mentorship, career preparation, and team leadership by participating in the SAAC and/or mentoring Rising Warhawks. Veteran Warhawks practice their mentorship skills with incoming freshmen. Finally, seniors who complete required program components graduate from the WLA with a Leadership Academy Certificate. Both juniors and seniors help to plan and execute Warhawk Outreach events.

While the WLA was designed at the macro level to support student development in a broad manner, one specific deficiency that the institution sought to address with the program was a decline in male student-athletes' average GPA (NCAA Division III does not utilize APR) over recent years. In addition, the athletic department and university leaders were also concerned with overall trends in the enrollment and retention of first-generation college students. At the same time that ideas for the WLA were being generated, a previous support position (the Associate Athletic Director for Student Services) was not retained due to budget and fiscal constraints. The reorganization presented an opportunity for growth.

Development of the Data-Driven Warhawk Leadership Academy Model

To further understand how to organize a comprehensive support services model, the researchers engaged in one-on-one interviews with head coaches comprising the Warhawk Leadership Academy Coaches Council (WLA Coaches Council). This group was specifically charged by the director of athletics to develop a holistic approach to support services expanding upon current campus-based programs. Coaches met monthly with the director of leadership development during the 2017–2018 academic year. Initial conversations centered on a needs assessment from the coaches' standpoint. Mid-year conversations turned to the development of a strategic plan for integration guided by an ecological model. Finally, these discussions resulted in the development of a group coined the "High

Performance" working group comprising campus health services, athletic department representatives, university faculty, and student-athletes. This group demonstrates an intentional form of high-impact practice and is in line with the institutional commitment to high-impact student support practices.

Specifically, the High Performance group that resulted from the WLA Coaches Council meetings was charged to meet monthly with the director of leadership development to streamline communication with respect to mental health, wellness, academic services, career and leadership development, and athletic performance. This group comprised senior leaders on campus employed by the University Health and Counseling Services faculty in the Department of Health, Physical Education, Recreation, and Coaching, (HPERC), and athletic department staff. In addition to the High Performance group, the director of leadership development met monthly with the SAAC executive board, an official leadership and governance body within the athletic department, to identify needs from the student-athletes' perspective. The researchers compared and contrasted needs assessments across campus constituents, athletic department employees, and student-athletes.

Building from the development of the High Performance group, the researchers, three tenure-track faculty members in the Department of HPERC, met bi-monthly to develop a data-driven approach to programmatic design. This is where the themes and critical success factors identified in the literature and information gathered from interview and focus groups were incorporated into an ecological model. The researchers continued to revise the model throughout the spring semester based on interview and focus group feedback, with an official unveiling for the following school year.

Genesis of a Student-Athlete Development Position

Seeking a fresh direction to best support student-athletes, the founding organizers sought creative and innovative collaboration across campus—including faculty—to intentionally develop a cluster of programs with student-athletes at the center of practice. The collaborative and innovative thinking, coupled with support from the chancellor, gave birth to the WLA as well as a new Division of Student-Athlete Engagement. Dr. Navarro, a member of the NCAA Yearly Initiatives Action Team, was charged by Director of Athletics Edmonds to create a student-athlete development program that would be collaborative, comprehensive in scope, and that would reframe and refocus what had formerly existed as traditional life skills programming. In addition to providing substantive support on the

UW-Whitewater campus, the founders also had a broader vision for the program. They saw the opportunity to create the first-ever NCAA Division III credit-based Leadership Academy, one that drew on partnerships with campus and faculty units, and that could be "exported" to be adopted or adapted by other Division III institutions.

Program Administration and Staffing

The WLA is a partnership between the Department of HPERC and School of Graduate Studies, and draws staffing resources from both units. The unit is supported by ten graduate practicum students and four undergraduate interns who assist in delivering multiple aspects of the program. At the beginning of each academic year the graduate coordinator works with the athletic department on site placement. Students undergo an interview process with the director of the Leadership Academy. They are able to earn up to three credits for their experience. Typically, these individuals work 20 hours a week in the evenings. Each individual functions as a member of the WLA Administrative Team which plans and executes individual components of the academy's program. The following is a list of administrative team roles:

- Coordinator of Warhawk Outreach (one intern)
- Coordinator of the Warhawks Give Back Program (one intern)
- Coordinator of Community Engagement and School-Based Programs (one intern)
- Coordinator of the Warhawk Awards: Showcase of Student-Athlete Excellence (one intern)
- Coordinator of Athletics Tutorial Service Program (one graduate student)
  - Graduate Student Tutors (nine).

The academy also seeks regular and substantive input from student-athletes to guide its operations. To ensure regular input the WLA director oversees the SAAC and WLA executive board, consisting of 17 student-athletes. Open communication between WLA leadership and the student-athletes keeps the athletes' needs front and center, as well as responsive to changes that may be needed.

Many of the educational, exploratory, or developmental sessions and experiences provided to student-athletes by the WLA are also facilitated or taught by staff from already established programs. Collaborations with campus partners allow the program to draw on talent, expertise, and resources from across the university.

Campus Collaborations

From its inception, the WLA was envisioned as an interdisciplinary collaboration across multiple student service units at UW-Whitewater. That broad vision was rooted in an understanding that student-athletes' needs and interests are diverse, and that the WLA would be more successful if its partnerships included as broad a range of perspectives and opportunities for student-athletes as possible. Specific collaborative units include:

- Department of Intercollegiate Athletics
- University Health and Counseling Services
- Career and Leadership Development
- Academic Advising and Exploration Center
- Academic Support/Tutoring Center
- Center for Students with Disabilities
- Multicultural Student Services Center
- Pathways Program and Diversity Leadership Certificate
- First-Year Experience Program
- Learning Communities
- Global Education.

The WLA partners with each of these campus units to provide resources to student-athletes. In the case of University Health and Counseling Services and Academic Support/Tutoring Services, both units offer additional open hours to meet the needs of student-athletes who are not typically able to utilize services during normal times. The First-Year Experience seminar and Learning Communities programs have worked with athletics to identify specific sections that are compatible with student-athletes' competition schedules. For their part, Multicultural Student Services and Global Education have worked with the WLA to develop programming and study abroad opportunities in the off season, or in condensed two- to three-week segments to enable student-athlete participation. From its inception the WLA staff have worked intently with campus partners on innovative ways to identify and provide resources and campus-based services seldom available to student-athletes.

Curriculum

The WLA curriculum and programming begin in the freshman year and build toward the senior year experience in recognition that campuses throughout the University of Wisconsin System—including UW-Whitewater—participate in the American Association of Colleges and

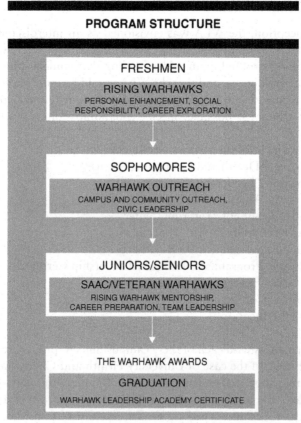

Figure 5.2a Warhawk Leadership Academy Program Structure

Universities' (AAC&U) Liberal Education and America's Promise initiative (LEAP), and the WLA curriculum builds off of LEAP's high-impact practice objectives. Figure 5.2a shows the Warhawk Leadership Academy Program Structure and Figure 5.2b shows the Warhawk Leadership Academy Curriculum Model.

Definitions

Personal Enhancement. A focus on personal enhancement provides a foundation for student-athlete success and the work of the WLA. This includes emphasizing personal identity, values, well-being, transition, and reflection.
Social Responsibility. Social engagement serves as a cornerstone through emphasis on social awareness, civic engagement, and moral application.
Career Development. Career development is a second cornerstone and is emphasized to assist student-athletes with career exploration, choice, preparation, and transition.

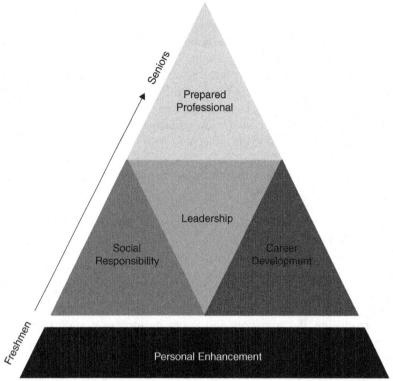

Figure 5.2b Warhawk Leadership Academy Curriculum Model

Leadership. Leadership represents the keystone of the curriculum's focus on developing student-athletes' personal, social, and professional leadership skills.
Prepared Professional. The WLA curriculum also requires student-athletes to engage in intentional application and reflection of skills to inform their own personal identities and become ambassadors of the Warhawk family.
SAAC. The SAAC engages all program areas, serves as a voice, and provides insight into the student-athlete experience.

Emerging Leaders Program: Identity Development for Student-Athletes

During the first semester of the year, the WLA curriculum requires student-athletes to participate in eight intentional credit-based sessions, which are administered as part of UW-Whitewater's New Student Seminar course. All freshmen complete this seminar designed to transition students to the campus environment. The WLA, however, enlarges and extends the content of these sessions by applying the concepts to the lives of student-athletes.

These sessions are a key component of the campuses' high-impact practices and LEAP standards. Each session is intentionally designed for freshman student-athletes and content focuses on mentorship (mentoring by Veteran Warhawks) and orientation to campus. The experiences serve as an extension of the campus-wide new student seminar and are offered as a one-credit experience through the College of Education and Professional Studies (CIGENRL 180: Identity Development of Student-Athletes). Individual sessions are delivered in conjunction with/by staff of WLA's campus partners and include the following concepts:

1. Warhawk nutrition and sports performance
2. Academic excellence
3. Student-athlete welfare
4. Mental health/nutrition
5. Social responsibility
6. Personal branding and career exploration.

Each of these sessions draws specifically on the relationship with campus and athletic department partners. In Session 1, the WLA specifically focuses on introducing the nutrition and sport performance staff to student-athletes. Session 2 introduces campus-based tutorial services and academic support with respect to class selection, academic planning, and selection of major. Sessions 3–4 focus on campus partnerships with University Health and Counseling Services and the Department of HPERC with faculty who specialize in sport psychology. Session 5 features an introduction to the mission of the SAAC and the Warhawks Give Back Community Outreach program. Finally, Session 6 begins to introduce the importance of major selection and personal branding and draws on expertise of the campus career and leadership development arm. Sessions are scheduled on Monday and Tuesday evenings, based on student-athlete availability (the WLA Coaches Council and SAAC identified these evenings as the best for programming).

Academic Excellence Sessions. Throughout both the fall and spring semesters of their first year in school, the WLA provides the student-athletes four hours of structured study sessions per week. These session times are chosen by the head coach and facilitated by the WLA graduate student staff. This partnership represents a significant collaboration with campus tutorial services and is available to all 20 sport programs participating in the Warhawk Leadership student-athlete engagement sessions. Academic Excellence study sessions are typically required for freshman student-athletes and then are optional based on coach policy for sophomores through seniors. The main impetus for creation of the Academic Excellence program was to take additional responsibility off the coach's plates at the Division III level as there are no academic advisors internal to athletics.

Warhawk Outreach: Campus and Community Outreach and Civic Leadership

During the sophomore year, the WLA curriculum steps back from course/session-based developmental opportunities to provide student-athletes the chance to practice leadership, outreach, and civic engagement in the community.

Warhawks Give Back Program. The WLA and SAAC partner to facilitate community and campus outreach efforts, in a program called Warhawks Give Back. The student-athletes are given the opportunity and resources to plan, organize, and participate in several events in the community and on campus. Specific community outreach initiatives include Reading, Moving, and Learning with the Warhawks and are the main component of this program. Student-athletes travel to local elementary schools to participate in physical education and literacy events with the young students.

Veteran Warhawks Program: Career Development Strategies for Student-Athletes

During the junior and senior years, student-athletes have the opportunity to participate in an additional eight educational sessions for student-athletes, this time focused on leadership development and preparation for life after athletics. While these are not mandatory sessions, typically each sport has representation in the upper level of the academy. Coaches specifically endorse participation in this upper-level opportunity. Sessions are again delivered through an additional one-credit course, and are provided by the College of Education and Professional Studies (CIGENRL 490: Career Strategies for Student-Athletes). The eight sessions include:

1. Career and Professional Development Strategies
2. DISC Assessment
3. Financial Planning
4. Employment Strategies I: Relationships
5. Employment Strategies II: The Search
6. Alumni Engagement Panel: Interviewing Strategies; Mock Interviews
7. Mental Health and Wellness
8. Life Beyond the Game.

In Session 1, student-athletes are introduced to long-term career planning and links between their current major and internship or career choices. Session 2 utilizes a personal assessment tool from the NCAA to identify personal behavioral strengths and weaknesses. Session 3 introduces the importance of personal budgeting and development as student-athletes begin to function with their own insurance, pay off school loans, and enter the world of work. Sessions 4 and 5 leverage relationships with program supporters and campus partners as alumni and company representatives come in to discuss developing relationships and the job search. In Session 6, alumni from the program help the younger student-athletes practice skills learned in sessions 4 and 5 as they work to create their elevator pitch. Alumni are happy to support current student-athletes and look to this opportunity as a way to give back. Finally, sessions 7 and 8 focus on personal health and well-being as student-athletes face retirement from sport and life beyond the game.

The Warhawk Awards: Awards Ceremony, Graduation, and the WLA Certificate

At the culmination of the senior year, student-athletes who have completed each level of the academy (Rising Warhawks, Warhawks Give Back, and Veteran Warhawks) are eligible to receive a WLA certificate. This certificate is given at the Warhawk Awards ceremony which celebrates student-athlete academic and co-curricular engagement efforts. At this event, corporate partners present Veteran Warhawks with a senior gift and graduation stole to commemorate their experience as a student-athlete. Student-athletes are encouraged to wear this stole at the campus graduation ceremony.

Program Evaluation

In recognition of the central role academics play in WLA's mission to prepare student-athletes for success in athletics, academics, and life, a tenure-track faculty member was also charged with the assessment and evaluation of the programs from the onset. In this case, assessment of the program also helped to fuel that faculty member's research agenda. The goal of the assessment study was to investigate how the WLA directly influences student-athletes' mental health and wellness, academic development, civic engagement, personal enhancement, and career preparation for life after athletics.

From the outset, the assessment plan was developed to privilege and learn from the student-athlete voice. The following research assessment questions guided the project:

RQ1 – What challenges do contemporary NCAA Division III student-athletes face as they transition to college?
RQ2 – How do contemporary NCAA Division III student-athletes navigate their transition to college with respect to their dual identity as both a student and athlete?
RQ3 – How, if at all, do NCAA Division III student-athletes respond to intentional leadership development training to:
a) enhance mental health and wellness?
b) promote academic engagement?
c) facilitate personal development as both a student and athlete?
d) foster major and career exploration?
e) enhance career readiness?
f) facilitate community relationships?
g) develop campus relationships?

Assessment Data Collection

The research team employed a mixed-methods approach to collecting data and evidence. During the fall semester, freshman student-athletes in the Rising Warhawks program (n=260) completed a pre- and post-treatment survey that was analyzed for face and content validity screening by a panel of experts. The survey collected information prior to and after student-athletes participated in formal WLA fall mentorship activities. This survey included a Likert scale self-assessment asking student-athletes to rate their awareness of and experiences with the following domains of leadership development and engagement on a college campus: (a) mental health and wellness, (b) academic engagement, (c) personal development, (d) major and career exploration, (e) career development, and (f) campus/community engagement opportunities.

The survey was administered via Qualtrics survey and all protocols and instruments were approved by the institution's IRB. The research team strove for a response rate of at least 60%. The pre- and post-test treatment included questions guided by the NSSE survey "high-impact practices" evaluation instrument and included additional questions developed by the research team.

Upon completion of the first semester of the WLA, Rising Warhawk and Veteran Warhawk participants were invited to participate in a semi-structured focus group interview. Focus group topics complemented questions posed and were informed by responses received in the survey. The research team employed purposeful sampling in order to garner focus group participants. The researchers proceeded with a guiding standard of at least 20 respondents (i.e., a minimum of five mentors and 15 mentees) for the focus group.

During the spring semester, as programming shifted to focus on Veteran Warhawks. These student-athletes completed an additional pre- and post-test treatment focused on perceptions of career preparation, career readiness, and leadership development. Student-athletes in the Veteran Warhawks program were asked to complete surveys via e-mail prior to Session 1 and after Session 8 of spring Veteran Warhawks programming. The Veteran Warhawks were likewise invited to participate in a semi-structured focus group interview which again employed a purposeful sampling technique with a guiding standard of at least 20 respondents comprising only Veteran Warhawks.

Data Analysis

Quantitative data analysis included descriptive statistics of the population sample as well as statistical differences between pre- and post-test responses. Qualitative data was transcribed using the assistance of a secure transcription service. To ensure accuracy in transcription, the research team performed member checks by providing detailed transcripts to focus group participants. Once all transcripts were amended and/or approved, the research team carried out systemic and comprehensive data analysis.

Qualitative data analysis included independent coding of the transcribed interviews by three members of the research team in order to develop process and pattern codes. These codes were triangulated and condensed to develop a conceptual model demonstrating an aggregate summation of findings for both the Rising Warhawks and Veteran Warhawks programs.

Program Outcomes

In recognition of the program's comprehensive and innovative approach, including its successful implementation, the WLA received the 2016 National Association of Collegiate Directors of Athletics (NACDA) N4A Model Practice Award, as well as the 2015 NASPA: Student Affairs Professionals in Higher Education Innovation Program Award. In addition, the university received a prestigious and sought-after national Carnegie classification for community engagement as a result of WLA's community outreach efforts.

On a programmatic level, since implementation, the average GPAs of student-athletes is higher than the general campus body. Likewise, retention and graduation rates of male student-athletes in the football and basketball programs has improved. Moreover, male student-athlete participation in SAAC and Leadership Academy programming increased by 47% from Year 1 to 3. Finally, the number of student-athletes participating in the program increased significantly:

- Veteran Warhawks Year 1: 32
- Veteran Warhawks Year 2: 55
- Rising Warhawks Year 1: 30
- Rising Warhawks Year 2: 160
- Participation in study tables enhanced from ten to 16 teams
- Participation in the Warhawks Give Back programming and events increased from 15 to 20 sport programs.

Quantitative and qualitative data suggested that participants experienced enhanced awareness of campus engagement opportunities, employer opportunities, community outreach opportunities, undergraduate major opportunities, mental health and wellness resources, and balancing student and athlete roles/identities. The program has proven itself to be sustainable, is supported by the chancellor, and is slated to continue.

Potential for Adaptation

The primary goal of this program was to develop a comprehensive and holistic NCAA Division III student-athlete support program model that would be successful for the students at UW-Whitewater. At the same time, its designers and founders had a vision that their work and planning could be used as a guiding model for other institutions. To date, UW-Whitewater has worked with 25 other institutions to implement similar programming tailored to each specific campus.

What is more, the program can be adopted, adapted, and implemented across NCAA divisions due to its focus on campus collaborations. Resources are perpetually scarce, and do not exist in isolation. The WLA program as described has operated on a budget of $35–40,000 per year. At UW-Whitewater, a significant portion of the budget is dependent upon private philanthropic efforts, and the model is likely highly appealing to both corporate partners and donors interested in philanthropic activity. In turn, universities might focus efforts on developing relationships with their development, athletic communications, and fan engagement offices as potential funding sources. A brief plan for development and implementation is depicted below.

Steps for Implementation

The success of this model program began with the voice of the SAAC, who led the charge, and provided substantial energy. To this end, each campus is able to begin the process, building from the infrastructure that already exists. We recommend the following steps:

Year 1 Focus

Budget

Identify creative funding opportunities:
- Work with campus partners to co-fund positions, speakers, programming
- Examine partnerships with outside grant agencies and forge faculty partnerships; apply to these opportunities

Relationships

Focus on further developing campus relationships with:
- First-Year Experience
- Student affairs units
- Academic affairs unit
- Office of Institutional Research
- Often, budgets for these units will assist with program startup.

Assessment

Develop assessment strategies, identify, and agree upon metrics for success, and ensure tools and instruments are planned for alongside and concurrent with curricular and programming development (see Chapter 6).
- Develop a comprehensive assessment plan that addresses all aspects of programming
- Partner with campus office of institutional research or a member of the faculty with expertise
- Plan both formative and summative assessments to guide implementation and measure outcomes.

Curriculum

- Begin with the SAAC as a pilot group to develop programs guided by the student-athlete voice
- Draw on contemporary frameworks with already developed and tested best practices.

Communication

- Develop relationships with the development office, athletic communications, and marketing to share message externally.

Year 2 Focus

Curriculum and Buy-In

- Pilot programming with SAAC
- Focus on campus collaborations with faculty members who have interest in teaching and co-facilitating
- Begin formal curricular processes to add credited components to the academic catalogue
- Target coaches of larger programs to lead the charge
- Continue leaning on the SAAC to champion efforts
- Work with corporate partners and donors to enhance giving levels.

Year 3 Focus

Curriculum

- Finalize the curricular process with faculty on campus; solidify courses and programs.

Assessment

- Continue to refine the assessment process
- Work closely with FAR, athletic board, and faculty researchers to refine the process
- Goals:
  - Demonstrate the value the program provides campus and athletics for recruitment (Division I)
  - Demonstrate value to enrollment (Division III and smaller schools).

Staffing Plan

- Work to grow and/or adjust full time employment (FTE) and staffing model as needed
  - Schools with smaller resources can develop an organizational structure that leverages undergraduate and graduate program support
  - Larger schools can work to enhance FTE through additional budget lines.

Challenges and Obstacles to Program Implementation

With the WLA, as is the case on any college campus, funding is the largest obstacle to sustain programming. To overcome this obstacle, the AD and the

Associate AD for Student-Athlete Development and Strategic Partnerships worked closely with the development office to develop a stable, long-term endowment model for the program. This included a targeted plan to approach potential donors interested in philanthropic efforts. In addition, staff worked closely with corporate partners to identify entities who/that find value in working with programs that support student-athletes. For example, many corporate partners desired the ability to share employment opportunities with student-athletes and saw the WLA as an entry point into this relationship.

An additional obstacle was a stifled relationship between campus and the athletic department due to recent athletics success. To enhance relations between campus and the athletic department, the WLA staff actively engaged with individuals across campus to educate faculty and staff about the Warhawk Leadership Academy and its mission to prepare student-athletes for excellence in academics and life after athletics. In turn, faculty found this an avenue for enhanced collaboration and launch pad for high-impact practice programs.

In the future, UW-Whitewater plans to continue to institutionalize the program by developing permanent course numbers in the College of Education and Professional Studies for all programming. In addition, staff continue to work closely with the first-year experience office and career and leadership development office on joint assessment measures to track enrollment and retention data for first-generation and under-represented students.

The program continues to focus on developing curricula to parallel campus efforts in support of the Carnegie community engagement classification. Members of the leadership team continue to serve on campus task forces to enhance faculty and campus buy-in. Meanwhile, UW-Whitewater continues to forward its targeted LEAP initiatives that focus on engaging student-athletes in the community, region, and globally.

While this program is the first of its kind in Division III, it is dependent upon the ability of a university to bring together academic and athletic departments strategically. The root of relationships begins with strategic communication and a willingness to share resources. In the case of UW-Whitewater, the partnership between the division of graduate studies and athletics allowed the graduate students who seek career experience in academic advising and career development to have meaningful opportunities to apply their skills with student-athletes. This model likely will require adaptation at Division III institutions which do not support graduate programs.

Implications

The WLA model was developed with the goal of realizing a more coordinated approach to student-athlete support services available to student-athletes on campus, which is key in schools and universities whose systems of support and care are decentralized, siloed and, thus, uncoordinated and less effective in fully supporting student-athletes. The WLA model depicts the approach needed using the levels of support and care that integrates student-athlete well-being. Through education and promotion practitioners can work to: 1) increase knowledge of support services; 2) increase access to support services; and 3) increase utilization of support services by student-athletes on campus, while 4) decreasing stigma (misconceptions and negative attitudes) associated with seeking help from support services, especially among student-athlete populations. In so doing, this provides centralized, holistic, coordinated, and, thus, more effective education, prevention, and intervention strategies across all levels of mental, physical, and social support issues that may occur and/or persist in the lives of student-athletes.

SUMMARY OF PROGRAM MODELS ACROSS DIVISIONS

From all three cases, there is a clear theme of collaborative efforts for each of these program models to achieve success for students and operate smoothly. While each institution faces different situations with financial support, collaborating across campus and even within the community brings in more resources and opportunities for programming. The focus on holistic student development is also evident from each of the models. Though the Division II and Division III cases show creative ways of offering student-athlete services with a limited budget, both WCU and UW-Whitewater offer a credit-based course for student-athletes that Nebraska does not. Different aspects of programming and modes of collaborating from these three models may be options for institutions in all NCAA divisions and within other governing bodies. These programming models are successful at these institutions based on a design that was built internally, based on what the students need at each institution, the available resources, and the connections made across campus units to offer different programs and structures for student-athletes. In Chapter 6, assessment is introduced as an important effort to ensure programs effectively encompass intended goals and outcomes for student-athletes.

REFERENCES

Adler, P., & Adler, P. (1987). Role conflict and identity salience: College athletics and the academic role. *Social Science Journal, 24*(2), 443–450.

Harrison, C. K., & Lawrence, S. M. (2003). African American student athletes' perceptions of career transition in sport: A qualitative and visual elicitation. *Race, Ethnicity and Education, 6*(4), 373–394.

Hodes, J. S., James, T., Martin, G., & Milliner, K. (2015). Go for the win: A collaborative model for supporting student-athletes. *The Learning Assistance Review, 20*(1), 47–60.

Nebraska Athletics. (2018a). *Goals for Evaluation.* Lincoln, NE : Nebraska Athletics

Nebraska Athletics. (2018b). *Post-eligibility Opportunities Program: Setting the Standard for Life beyond Athletics.* Lincoln, NE: Nebraska Athletics.

NU Athletic Communications. (2017, January 6). *Post-eligibility opportunities overview.* Retrieved from www.huskers.com/ViewArticle.dbml?DB_OEM_ID=100&ATCLID=210245693

NU Athletic Communications. (2018, April 9). *Herman Student Life Complex.* Retrieved from www.huskers.com/ViewArticle.dbml?DB_OEM_ID=100&ATCLID=1513079

Chapter Six

Assessment and Data-Driven Practices in Intercollegiate Athletics

Assessment has taken an increasingly central role across higher education as colleges and universities have sought to ensure that the range of experiences they provide their students are meaningful, effective, and maintain fidelity to their goals and missions (Schuh, 2009). As they have begun embracing assessment practices in their pursuit of quality programs and learning environments, institutions have shifted away from the simplistic view that, in order to authentically assess the quality of the experiences they offer, they must invest money in educational experiences (Astin, 1985). Instead, a new breed of assessment professional has emerged who is qualified to evaluate and identify any need for new roles, practitioners, or office functions, and recent decades have seen the rapid proliferation of these professionals in all sectors of higher education (Kuh, Jankowski, Ikenberry, & Kinzie, 2014). Today's assessment professionals bring with them a host of frameworks, approaches, and evaluative skills for appraising student learning and development in the diverse contexts students encounter in college. Moreover, assessment helps educational leaders by providing insights, understanding, and the data necessary to drive decision-making.

It is no surprise, perhaps, that the assessment movement has come to athletics. In fact, given the role that athletic programming plays in mediating the student-athlete experience, ensuring that intercollegiate athletes are provided with well-engineered, high-impact programming and experiences that enhance their outcomes is paramount. As illustrated elsewhere in this book, institutional programming touches every aspect of the student-athlete experience in college. Traditional in-class academics are often mediated by policies and programming that can limit the types and times of courses student-athletes pursue. Likewise, tutoring and supplemental instruction, among other programs, change how student-athletes access their coursework and engage in learning. Co-curricular activities impact the kinds of engagement experiences in which student-athletes participate outside of class. Common developmental programming (including identity and career exploration workshops or classes), leadership training and practice opportunities, participation in interventions targeting behavioral pitfalls such as drinking or substance abuse as well as those promoting desirable behaviors such as studying, networking, and time management, are all woven together to support intercollegiate athletes. At the same time, they also ensure that student-athletes have one of the most engineered, curated, and mediated college experiences among all types of students in higher education today. It is no great leap to conclude that given the high degree to which student-athletes' college experiences are "programmatized," that all stakeholders, including institutional leaders, athletic department professionals, faculty, practitioners, and student-athletes themselves have a vested interested in ensuring that those programs are effective.

The sheer amount of programming that impacts student-athletes' college experience provides a compelling rationale for practitioners to engage in regular assessment to ensure the programs, in fact, work. It is critical for leaders to determine whether their programs are actually forwarding the goals and outcomes they are designed to promote. There are, however, additional reasons to engage in regular assessment and assessment-related practices in athletics. As with most areas of programming in higher education, budgets for new approaches, staffing, and experiences are limited, and with many student-athletes in need, support units must accomplish lofty goals with what is often insufficient resources. New and innovative programs must demonstrate their value to receive or maintain funding from administrative leaders.

Further, in a rationale that is likely unique to student-athlete support units, programs must often ensure that their practices are in line with the NCAA and other governing bodies that impose strict, and sometimes shifting, rules and regulations that must be followed while providing students proper information and education, as well as support for maintaining eligibility, persistence toward graduation, and development for their future after sport. Keeping up to date on changes and their implications for program practices can add an additional layer of challenge.

Taken together, these several reasons provide ample justification for practitioners to develop plans to collect evidence that their programming is working. This includes seeking both formative and summative feedback from student-athletes on a regular basis, as well as collecting outcomes data that can be used to improve programming.

WHAT IS ASSESSMENT?

Scholars in the field of assessment, as in any discipline, maintain a spirited dialogue over the purpose(s), scope, and terms used to define the field, as well as over its most critical and central practices. One recognized leader in the field, Linda Suskie, suggested that the main focus of assessment is "student learning," (Suskie, 2004) and that assessment practices should focus primarily on whether and how students learn defined content or skills. Others broaden the definition by employing a more inclusive description: "Assessment is the systematic collection, review, and use of information about educational programs for the purpose of improving student learning and development" (Banta & Palomba, 2014, p. 1). Banta and Palomba's definition may be a more useful one in the context of assessment in intercollegiate aspects given the importance that developmental theories play in programming for student-athletes and the distinctive challenges they face in their college careers (Nite, 2012).

For definitional purposes, we might further broaden the scope of assessment in intercollegiate athletics to include what might traditionally be termed "program evaluation" by adding a deliberate focus on the processes related to, implementation of, and effectiveness at achieving specified outcomes within the myriad resources, programs, and services institutions create and provide to support their student-athlete populations. Further, given the distinctive space student-athletes navigate in the nexus of institutions' revenue-using and revenue-generating activities, it is important to recognize that assessment in intercollegiate athletics can include a financial focus in ways that mirror traditional student affairs programming assessment ("justify your existence"), but that is less prevalent than that of strictly academic programming and the assessment of learning outcomes.

Still, assessment, whether within or without intercollegiate athletics, has a purpose implied in its definition, but should perhaps be made more explicit as it speaks to how we operationalize assessment: not just what assessment is, but another aspect of its purpose. Specifically, the purpose of assessment is to collect evidence that a program or initiative is *meeting its articulated goals*. In this way, assessment is tightly tethered to specific and articulated objectives, not vague goals or desires. These objectives are typically defined by the program which has, in turn, been designed with policies and practices in mind that should promote those objectives. In sum, the purpose of assessment activities is to collect evidence that a program is delivering on what it claims to do, or what it is designed to do.

It is also important to note that assessment in intercollegiate athletics carries with it a number of formidable challenges beyond those seen in other areas of higher education assessment. Davis (1987) outlined four challenges to consider. First, athletics organizations engender intense feelings and passion that can militate against close examination of practices. Second, as many support programs in athletics are idiosyncratic, that is, they are distinctive to their institutional context, populations, culture, and programming, reliable comparative information for benchmarking is difficult. Third, athletics is big business, and the influence of money can dissuade leaders from conducting too close an examination and revealing imperfections. Finally, athletics programs develop and administer programming, including policies and practices that are often mandated by governance structures at the conference, regional, and national levels. In-depth and summative evaluation of such practices has the potential to reveal how programs may not be meeting mandated levels of performance, or ways in which they do not accurately reflect programmatic missions or goals (Davis, 1987).

An additional challenge to conducting assessment in intercollegiate athletic programming is related to how and where institutions typically allocate their assessment expertise resources, as well as the dominant and segregated model of how student-athlete support programs are often administered. Assessment professionals and their offices are most often housed within the academic affairs branch of administration, providing them little access, nor a mandate to obtain student-athlete data or outcomes data related to student-athlete support program practices. Still, such challenges should not deter institutions from pursuing meaningful assessment of the programs they offer their student-athletes. With buy-in from educational leaders, partnerships between various institutional offices and units, and a commitment to achieving excellence, institutions can create an environment that values assessment and what it can bring to the range of programs athletic departments develop. After all, practitioners can only determine whether program expectations are being met through systematic collection of evidence, analysis, and defined mechanisms to feed findings and data back into units to drive decision-making processes.

FINDINGS FROM ASSESSMENT IN ATHLETICS

Despite the challenges of conducting assessment activities in athletics, good work is underway in athletic departments and their partner programs at all levels across the country. In contrast to other well-developed disciplines and domains of inquiry, however, assessment studies are less frequently reflected in the literature. The relative paucity of published examples is the result of several conditions.

For one, assessment studies are conducted by institutions and programs for the purpose of continual improvement, not for generalizability or to contribute to the literature. Assessment studies eschew generalizability as an inquiry value, and often seek to understand programs and practices in situ, with little attention or energy paid to broader applicability. They also tend to focus on continual improvement, and emphasize the collection of formative information that can be used in decision-making, rather than conforming to traditional research norms. For these reasons, very few academic journals solicit single institution's studies, regardless of their rigor, for publication. Also, more often than not, assessment studies are not published at all in the traditional sense, but are instead issued for internal use only in the form of a report. It can be difficult to find copies of these reports on school websites, even at public institutions with policies favoring transparency. Further, athletic departments can have a culture of opacity and often jealously guard their data. In general, student data can be sensitive, and the addition of monetary implications, as well as the potential for intense and potentially intrusive media coverage, make many departments reluctant to permit publication. Finally, related to the issues of generalizability, assessment studies seek to reveal whether programs, initiatives, or interventions meet their *own* articulated goals, which may or may not be reflected in other contexts or at other institutions.

Still, time spent in the literature reveals that it reflects examples of assessment in student-athlete programming including individual program evaluations, initiatives, interventions, and even funding and organizational models. Often, these assessment studies skirt the line between academic research and program assessment. For example, Dudley, Johnson, and Johnson (1997) explored the impact that emphasizing cooperative learning environments and structures has when attempting to enhance student-athletes' academic and social experiences. Broughton (2001) and Broughton and Neyer (2001) described a comprehensive, holistic counseling program targeting student-athletes to support their psychoeducational development and life skills exploration through directed counseling sessions. Their reports outlined the strengths and weaknesses of the counseling program and provide recommendations for improving the outcomes of student-athletes utilizing the program's counseling services.

Career services and other career exploration programs are a significant part of the wraparound services offered student-athletes in contemporary support practices, and are likewise scrutinized to ensure they are of quality and meet outcome expectations. Petitpas, Danish, McKelvain, and Murphy (1992) reported on such a program designed for elite student-athletes and reveal opportunities for career counselors to strengthen the programming offered to the programs' student-athlete clientele.

Many institutional initiatives designed to address the distinctive needs of student-athletes are framed as interventions, often focused on health and wellness issues. At the same time, institutions have a vested and often pecuniary interest in ensuring these programs work as intended. Programmatic interventions have therefore been designed for student-athletes including to address heavy and binge-drinking behaviors (Doumas, Haustveit, & Coll, 2010; Thombs & Hamilton, 2002), substance abuse (Marcello, Danish, & Stolberg, 1989), and even criminal behaviors (Southall, 2001). Each of these reports describes program goals, outlines their approaches to measuring effectiveness, and then describes outcomes.

Broadening the scope of what can be described as a program within the world of athletics, institutions will often develop initiatives to leverage athletics and the highly valuable relationships between teams and their fans for financial benefit. Such programs, likewise, can be assessed for their effectiveness—do they generate revenue, and what are the best ways to leverage athletics to generate giving? Such programs, and their success, are explored by Baade and Sundberg (1996), and Stinson and Howard (2007).

Athletic departments are also often called upon to help address a wide array of institutional goals and initiatives. In practice, these are put into practice through institutional programs which, in turn, can be assessed for effectiveness and their impact on the institution's goals. Padgett and Reid (2002) described their evaluation of an institution-level program designed to increase diversity, through targeted support for student-athletes, in particular Black male athletes.

Finally, institutions can assess the effectiveness of their structures and organizations. Information from these types of assessments can provide much-needed information during restructuring initiatives. Researchers have approached the assessment of organizational aspects of athletic departments in a number of ways, including to describe models (Cunningham & Rivera, 2001; Schroeder, 2010; Slack & Parent, 2006), or through close analysis of leadership models and styles (Ryska, 2002).

DEVELOPING AN ASSESSMENT PLAN FOR ATHLETIC PROGRAMMING

Assessment in any context requires developing a plan and then following it. In the following sections, we will outline a basic plan or model for conducting assessment activities in the context of intercollegiate athletics, specifically through a fictitious leadership development program. It is important to note that the basic model is applicable to a wide variety of contexts, environments, and can be used to develop a plan for assessing many types of objectives across many types of programs. It should also be noted that this discussion refers to a "program." "Program" can refer to diverse types of programs, coursework, interventions, initiatives, and more. A program, in this context, is a set of activities that are designed to forward or support a set of objectives.

DATA PRACTICE IN INTERCOLLEGIATE ATHLETICS

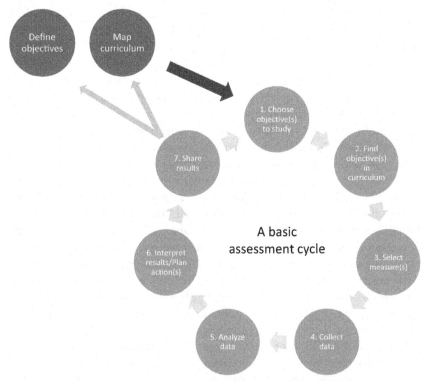

Figure 6.1 Basic Assessment Cycle

The Assessment Cycle

Before discussing the individual components of a basic assessment plan and how they fit together, it may be helpful to step back and examine the whole. Most models of assessment are based on a cyclic process. The cycle is a powerful organizing tool because it consists of discrete steps, each with its own component steps, but also because it communicates the ongoing, and iterative nature of assessment. In other words, working through the cycle should provide a program with valuable information that can be fed back into the program to either justify changes (strengthen or improve some aspect of the program) or validate that practices are meeting expectations and generating the expected outcomes. Figure 6.1 shows an example of a basic assessment cycle.

Defining Objectives

The most important activity in any assessment plan or process is the first: defining objectives. It is critical to establish quality objectives, and articulating them should precede entry into the formal assessment cycle. Objectives are statements of the knowledge, skills, habits of mind, development, and other factors that a program seeks to forward. These objectives can be cognitive, affective, developmental, or organizational, to name a few. These objectives, or their achievement, are what an assessment study seeks to measure. Have the objectives been met by participants of the program? To what degree? If they have not been met, or have not been met to the degree expected or desired by the program, why not? These important questions cannot be addressed without an articulated statement of the basic objective.

Across assessment practice these objectives can be called a variety of names including Program Learning Objectives (PLOs), Student Learning Objectives (SLOs), Course/Certificate Learning Objectives (CLOs), Developmental Learning Objectives (DLOs), Institutional Learning Objectives (ILOs), or simply Learning Objectives (LOs). Nomenclature depends on the context and scope of the objectives. Also worth noting is that practitioners often use the terms "objective" and "outcome" somewhat interchangeably. While "outcome" entails a slightly more summative perspective than the aspirational "objective," either is sufficient for discussing sets of knowledge, skills, habits of mind, or development a program wants participants to achieve.

In a perfect world, a program's objectives will have been defined prior to the program having been implemented. Moreover, the best objectives are developed through collaborative processes that draw upon the perspectives of all relevant stakeholders. In the case of intercollegiate athletic programming, this could include student-athletes, coaches, support staff, program practitioners, athletic departments, faculty, administration, and educational leaders. It is likewise appropriate for organizations such as NCAA and N4A to provide guidance and insight in the development of program objectives as well.

Objectives can be diverse but must be specific, measurable, and achievable. For example, many programs seek to promote leadership qualities in student-athletes. A poorly worded objective from such a program might state that "Participants in the program will know how to lead." While it may be possible to extrapolate what this means, it is actually rather vague, and "know how" can be difficult to measure. It could be phrased much better, as in "Program participants will demonstrate common leadership characteristics," or "Program graduates will apply leadership strategies to real-world problems and scenarios." The first example would be challenging to measure; the second iterations, however, clearly imply what would be measured, namely the participant's demonstration of some agreed-upon qualities of leadership or their application to challenges. Well-written objectives can be seen as eliciting a demonstration of the desired objection.

If the objective is not clear as written, it can likely be rephrased for clarity and to make it more measurable.

Most programs should have a short set of articulated objectives, and programs that have dozens are unlikely to be able to forward more than a handful legitimately. Too many objectives signify programming that is likely too watered down or ineffective. Programs may have additional sets of objectives that are related to, but somewhat outside of, the scope of a specific programmatic curriculum. Sometimes these are known as metrics or key indicators. Some of these can be defined by a program and institution, or by external organizations such as the NCAA. These metrics can be seen as proxies for formalized, discrete, and measurable LOs. The field has coalesced around a common set of performance metrics, including APR, GSR, Federal Graduation Rate (FGR), GPA, time-to-degree (semesters or quarters), and retention rates. Though often employed for reporting purposes, and despite a relationship with learning or development supported by the program, such metrics cannot speak to the success a program has at forwarding *particular* objectives.

Curriculum/Experience Map

The second major activity in developing an assessment plan is to map the curriculum. In this context, "curriculum" should be interpreted broadly to include the sets of activities and experiences through which a participant would move toward achievement of the objective. In an academic program, the curriculum would consist primarily of coursework and possibly some additional experiences or activities. In support programming the curriculum might include advising and counseling sessions, engagement opportunities, workshops, facilitated experiences, and more. Mapping the curriculum provides a window into where and when (in the sets of experiences and activities to which participants can be expected to be introduced) participants might practice, or demonstrate mastery or achievement of, a particular objective.

The example curriculum map shown in Table 6.1 describes a fictitious leadership development program that could easily resemble one provided for student-athletes. In this case, the curriculum consists of two listed courses, internship experiences, and a culminating portfolio project. Curriculum maps are most often presented as a matrix that crosses curricular elements (coursework, activities, experiences) with the program's LOs. The "Xs" in the intersections between the two represent the mapping, and "X," quite literally, marks the spot. Each X indicates opportunities in the curriculum that program designers have engineered to provide participants an opportunity to engage with the particular objective.

Table 6.1 Example Curriculum Map

	Objective 1: Apply leadership models in real-world situations	Objective 2: Apply communication strategies to lead groups	Objective 3: Apply gathered information to problems in leading
LEAD 465: Contemporary Models of Leadership	X		X
LEAD 466: Communication in Leadership		X	X
Leadership internship	X	X	
Capstone reflective portfolio project	X	X	X

While this example map is basic in design and simply uses an X to indicate engagement of the objectives at particular moments in the curriculum, some curriculum maps will go further to indicate the level of engagement with indicators such as "I" for introductory, "P" for practice, and "D" for demonstrate mastery. There are numerous schemes in the assessment literature for representing levels of engagement, but a simple way to approach basic assessment planning is to consider each X as an opportunity for students to demonstrate some level of achievement of the objective.

In the example, the fictitious "LEAD 465: Contemporary Models of Leadership" can be seen as providing participants an opportunity to demonstrate achievement of LOs 1 and 3. In such a course, participants would likely be provided with materials and instruction designed to teach them models of leadership, and then require some type of project or other opportunity to apply such models to problems of leadership. In so doing, the participant could then demonstrate achievement of both objectives.

It is important to consider that simply because a map indicates that a particular curricular element *should* support a particular objective, the devil is in the details. If participants are not prompted to demonstrate achievement of the objective, then it should not be mapped in that way.

PLANNING A STUDY

Once a program has well-articulated objectives and a curriculum map, it is possible to design an assessment study, beginning with Step 1 of the cycle. If insufficient time has been devoted to developing objectives and a map, however, it is unlikely that program practitioners will be able to develop a successful assessment study and collect trustworthy evidence that participants are meeting objectives.

Choose an Objective(s) (What to Assess)

The first step in the assessment cycle is to select an objective or objectives to assess. Depending upon the context, it may not be necessary to assess all of a program's LOs at once, every semester, or year. On the other hand, if the program consists of a relatively short set of experiences, such as a one-time workshop or event, the context may dictate that all objectives be assessed at once in order to ensure the program is meeting its goals.

If only one, or a smaller subset of objectives are to be assessed, it will be necessary to choose from among those available, and there are several rationales that can inform selection. Program administrators, faculty, practitioners, participants, or others may suggest focusing on a particular objective due to concerns over whether participants are achieving the objective at a desired level of performance. For example, if instructors in the example leadership program felt that recent participants had not been developing adequate communication skills or strategies, then Learning Objective #2 might be a good choice. Alternatively, some will simply assess objectives in order, select one that has not been assessed for some time, or select an objective that has synergy with another focus of the program, department, or institutional initiative at the time.

Find the Objective in the Curriculum (When to Assess)

Once an objective or objectives have been selected, it is time to determine advantageous opportunities to collect evidence of participants' achievement. This is where the curriculum map comes into play. It is relatively simple to consult the map to see in which courses, activities, or experiences participants engage with the selected objective, or where they would have the best opportunity to demonstrate achievement of the objective.

More often than not, the best opportunities will be toward the end of a curriculum rather than in initial or introductory portions. Capstone and culminating experiences, final activities or events, and other post-activity/experience opportunities frequently provide the best occasions to collect evidence. They are also, logically, the places in the curriculum where participants will have had the full benefit of all of the program's experiences and curriculum designed to develop the capacities delineated in the objective. Toward the end of the program, therefore, is typically the best place to collect evidence.

It is also important to consider another, deeper aspect of the curriculum when determining when and where to collect evidence. Direct assessment of participant performance provides the best evidence of achievement. In contrast, indirect assessment, while still a good source of data, provides a less trustworthy measure. As an example, a direct measure of performance of leadership communication skills might be a required presentation in the context of a leadership course. An indirect assessment might entail the same participant filling out a survey asking for ratings on personal leadership communication abilities. Seeing the performance in action and in person will almost always trump a participant's self-rating and perceptions.

When selecting an opportunity to collect evidence, it is also advisable to utilize opportunities that are already a part of the set of activities and experiences in the program, rather than adding an additional burden on participants and program administrators. In the example, evaluating participants' leadership communication abilities within the context of a presentation that is part of the program rather than adding an additional test, survey, or performance is preferable—it is less work for everyone, and participants often provide a more genuine performance (and even try harder) when the performance is integral to the experience than if it is an add-on for the purpose of assessment.

Select Measures (How to Assess)

There are many ways to measure achievement of an objective. Some have been discussed already. Direct measurement, rather than indirect measurement, is typically better. Assessing authentic performances is better than using contrived performances that are required only for assessment purposes. Aside from these basic guidelines, there are numerous ways to measure achievement of an objective. Most work products produced in the context of a curriculum are fair game. These can include papers, reflections, presentations, performances, tests, portfolios, surveys, inventories, interviews, and more. The most important aspect to consider is whether the work product is aligned with the objective in question. That is, the work will elicit a demonstration from the participant, but for the purposes of assessing a particular objective, it is essential that the demonstration elicited is the demonstration of the objective in question.

Quite often it is helpful to utilize a scoring guide, evaluation matrix, or rubric to aid in the assessment. For example, participants in a leadership communication course/workshop might be asked to give a presentation that would demonstrate their ability to utilize communication strategies common to good leaders. While giving the presentation, program facilitators could score the performance on a rubric to collect the necessary data. A simple rubric could prompt ratings of several criteria that are aligned with the communication strategies addressed in the program, such as having a strong thesis/message, providing argument/support, using eye contact, addressing questions, and so on.

Developing a simple rubric such as the example shown in Table 6.2 provides a number of distinct advantages. The rubric is able to convert the performance into a quantitative score that can then be combined with data from other participants' performances. In the example, the highest possible score is a 16, and if many participants' scores were combined in analysis, it would be possible to make programmatic claims such as "the average participant scored a 12.5/16 on the leadership communication presentation." This number could be compared to other cohorts, demonstrating potential trends over time.

Such rubrics also help to provide consistency across reviewers and over time; they help to remove subjectivity from the evaluation. Some rubrics will even include a prose description of what an "inadequate" vs "excellent" performance looks like in the context of a specific criterion. For example, perhaps an inadequate performance provided zero points of argument/support for a thesis, while an excellent performance provided five or more.

Scoring individual components also adds a diagnostic component to the analysis. Scoring of a cohort of participants using the example rubric might reveal that while the average total score was 12.5/16, the average

Table 6.2 Example Rubric

	Insufficient (1)	Developing (2)	Adequate (3)	Excellent (4)
Thesis/Message				
Argument/Support				
Eye contact				
Addresses questions				

score for "eye contact" might be 1.5/4. This would provide practitioners an opportunity to re-examine how the program conveys to participants the importance of eye contact, and they might revamp how that portion of their instruction is administered.

Rubrics can be used to score a wide range of performance types such as presentations, papers, reflections, and more. If the performance is a work product produced by a participant, whether something turned in, or presented live, it can likely be scored with a rubric. It is simply important that the criteria included in the rubric are aligned with the objective and speak to what various levels of achievement on that objective look like.

For other types of measures, tools like a rubric are not appropriate. A multiple-choice test, for example, is an inappropriate measure for a rubric. Likewise, many indirect measures such as surveys are not enhanced by using a rubric.

Collect Data

Collecting data is fairly straightforward. Data can be collected from individual participants, cohorts, or even combined over time. Data can also be collected from different time points in a curriculum to assess the same objective—perhaps different aspects of the objective—or to show growth. If collecting at multiple points, or in different settings, it may again be helpful to develop standardizing tools such as a rubric to ensure alignment and to maintain consistency. For example, participants in a leadership program might give a presentation early in the program, and later in the program. Using the same rubric to score both presentations will have the potential to show growth, and will ensure that the same criteria are being addressed at both timepoints.

Analyze Data

Data analysis is simply bringing together data points, reducing their volume, making sense of them, and then writing up a synopsis or summary to communicate the results to others. Analysis can take many forms including written synthesis of findings, mathematical computations, visualizations such as graphs, tables, or charts, or many other approaches. Analysis approaches will be dictated by the type of objectives being assessed, the types of measures used, and the skill and abilities of the analyst. Quite often analysis does not require high-level skills, but simply descriptive statistics, or clear and concise prose. A lucid description of what was revealed in an assessment study is far more important than advanced mathematics or fancy visualizations.

Interpret Results/Plan Action(s)

Once results have been derived, it is important to interpret them in the context of the program and the objectives of the program. How did participants perform? What were the expectations for their performance, and were those expectations met? If expectations were met, the implication is that the program is adequately supporting participants in developing the capacity to achieve the objective. If not, however, it is important to ask why.

With respect to setting expectations, it is important to consider that perfect performance is probably not a realistic or achievable standard in every context. On the example rubric, it might be acceptable for all participants (or 75% of participants) to score a 12 or above out of 16 in order to claim that the program is sufficiently supporting achievement of the objective. Sometimes it may take a few times conducting a particular assessment study to determine the most appropriate threshold or performance expectation. At some point, however, it will be important to set such a threshold or expectation so that statements can be made about whether the program is succeeding in its objectives.

Sometimes when performance expectations are not met, it is fairly easy to pinpoint the cause. Other times it may require repeating an assessment study several times—sometimes with tweaks in the study design—in order to isolate and reveal the cause of the failure. The tools used in the study may help that process. As in the previous example, if the study uses a rubric, program practitioners might find that participants were not meeting expectations, but had scored well across all criteria except for "eye contact." This would suggest that the program curriculum be adjusted to more explicitly or directly emphasize that particular skill/practice. The assessment could then be repeated with a new cohort and the new curriculum could be tested.

Likewise, on tests or surveys, various questions can be aligned with various program objectives. It is not unusual for program participants to excel in one area, and struggle in others. The pattern revealed by the assessment study can point to opportunities to adjust or strengthen the curriculum to better support the desired objectives.

In the assessment literature, this part of the process is often referred to as "closing the loop," and invokes a closing of the circle and coming back to the starting point. It is also the moment of the assessment process where data can inform decisions, whether about maintaining or changing aspects of the program.

Share Results

Finally, a critical component of the assessment cycle is to share results. Results can, and should, be shared with all of the major stakeholders of the program. Those same groups of people who helped to develop the LOs back at the beginning of the process should all be included. Results from assessment can be critical to programs for securing or maintaining funding. They can provide a rationale for expansion of programming, elimination of some aspects, or demonstrate to the wider community the value of the program and the experiences it offers.

CONCLUDING THE ASSESSMENT CYCLE

Completing the cycle is not the end of the process. The information gathered throughout the cycle may inform changes to the program, including revisions of the LOs or curriculum map. Most often, however, engaging in the assessment cycle can inform changes to materials, experiences, or activities offered by the program in ways that enhance the student experience. Assessment is sometimes referred to as a process of continual improvement, and while one cycle may conclude, it informs the next cycle, the next beyond that, and should be used to ensure that the program is supporting conditions in which program participants are able to achieve the objectives of the program.

ASSESSMENT PROGRAM MODEL: BOSTON UNIVERSITY

Boston University has been at the forefront of the field of assessment in intercollegiate athletics and has been developing a model for assessing several aspects of student-athlete development. In 2017, Boston University created the position of Director of Leadership and Career Development and recruited Dr. Marissa Nichols for the role. Nichols is a former student-athlete, campus SAAC president, and student-athlete development expert. In pioneering her new role, she immediately determined a needs assessment of the athletic department and its staff was paramount to forging a path for her student-athletes' success. She worked with her colleagues, gathering perspectives and values, and used the ongoing discussions to develop a set of departmental goals and objectives. Then, further using feedback gathered from administrators, staff, coaches, and students, she began to design programmatic components aligned with those objectives to support her students while meeting department and team goals based on both learning and developmental outcomes. These programmatic components became the "curriculum" of the department, and articulated the time points during which student-athletes were most directly supported in achieving departmental objectives.

The wide variety of initiatives she implemented required continual assessment, to determine their effectiveness, but also to shape their direction,

Fall 2017 Evaluation Summary
CAS FY 103: Developing Leaders – Identity, Performance, Social Responsibility

Method: This report summarizes the results of the pre- and post-evaluation students completed at the beginning and end of the inaugural one-credit class.

Areas of Assessment: The evaluations assessed student-athlete personal characteristics (leadership mindset, personality mindset, grit), curriculum effectiveness (knowledge / skill-attainment, self-reported behaviors), course satisfaction, and recommendations for future (post-only).

This course was compared to the effectiveness of the traditional three-session orientation.

Area of Assessment	Evaluation
About the Class	**Quick Stats:** • 49 first-year student-athletes enrolled / successfully passed based on course requirements • 16 of 24 BU Athletics teams represented • Four athletics staff administrators involved weekly (Marissa, Mindy, Eline, Heather) • Partnership with College of Arts and Sciences First Year Programming **Touchpoints with BU Campus (20 total):** • Center for Career Development (5); Center for Gender, Sexuality, & Activism (2); College of Arts and Sciences (3); Dean of Students (1); Office of the Ombuds (1); Questrom School of Business (2); School of Education (3); Sexual Assault Response & Prevention Center (1); Wellness & Prevention (2) **Touchpoints with BU Community (15 total):** • Alumni (3); One Love Foundation (6); Upperclassman (6) **Data-driven Content:** • Growth Mindset – Academics, Athletics, Personality, Leadership (Dweck) • StrengthsFinder 2.0 (Gallup) • Four-Year Career Plan • Mental Skills Training (Baltzell) • Engagement with faculty, alumni, campus constituents
Student-athlete Personal Characteristics	**About Personality Mindset:** Beliefs about one's personal characteristics / personalities. In a growth mindset, personality can be developed / shifted through effort and challenge. **Research Results:** For the one-credit course, there was a significant increase in Mindset scores (0.44 on a 7-point scale) with respect to personality ($p < 0.05$). For the other constructs, leadership mindset and grit, there was no difference.
Curriculum Effectiveness; Knowledge/skill-attainment	**Between the beginning and end of class:** • **Techniques / coping behaviors:** 1 in every 5 students reported an increase in one of the following techniques / coping behaviors: 1) mindfulness; 2) meditation; 3) working with a licensed professional (e.g., therapist, nutritionist); 4) expanding their peer or support group; or 5) building a relationship with a mentor • **Personal strengths:** There was a 100% increase in students feeling 'extremely knowledgeable / skilled' about their individual strengths • **Managing myself, time, and expectations:** There was an increase from 44% to 70% of students feeling 'extremely knowledgeable / skilled' or 'very knowledgeable / skilled' about self-management • **Campus resources:** There was a 66.61% increase in knowledge / skills about individuals or campus resources in place to support / enhance the student-athlete experience

Draft II: 01.16.18

Figure 6.2a Boston University Assessment Tool

so in her first year in the role she conducted formative and summative assessments by collecting evidence and data from a variety of sources, using different techniques. For example, students completed evaluations for each individual session they attended. Those data were analyzed in concert with other sources including engagement and participation metrics provided by student-athletes and administrators/staff/coaches of other campus programs, as well as conference/regional/national events, involvement in specific high-impact practices (e.g., a class Nichols designed for freshman student-athletes), and revenue sources (e.g., grant from the Patriot League for Boston University's Leadership Academy).

She tailored her survey instrument questions to examine students' acquisition of knowledge, skills, behaviors, and values. To Nichols, it is important that assessment practices speak to a variety of stakeholders, including

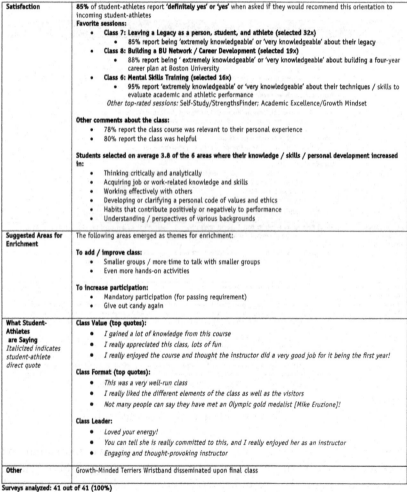

Figure 6.2b Boston University Assessment Tool (continued)

students, alumni, campus administration, and even employers. Data and analysis must connect to and align with the institution's mission, advance institutional effectiveness, frame beliefs about leadership, address strategic goals, and demonstrate improvement over time. Her overall analysis of the previous year's assessment activities included what she deemed growth points across a range of areas, focusing on: departmental, campus, and national engagement; effectiveness of sessions offered; curriculum enhancements; new initiatives; student learning; high-impact practices; and funding sources. Boston University's assessment tool is presented in Figure 6.2a and b.

The next chapter provides a case study of Rutgers University and its implementation of strategic partnerships and a leadership development program to enhance student-athlete holistic development.

REFERENCES

Astin, A. W. (1985). *Achieving Educational Excellence* (1st ed). San Francisco, CA: Jossey-Bass.

Baade, R. A., & Sundberg, J. O. (1996). Fourth down and gold to go? Assessing the link between athletics and alumni giving. *Social Science Quarterly*, *77*(4), 789–803.

Banta, T. W., & Palomba, C. A. (2014). *Assessment Essentials: Planning, Implementing, and Improving Assessment in Higher Education*. San Francisco, CA: Jossey-Bass.

Broughton, E. (2001). *Counseling and support services for college student athletes*. Paper presented at the Annual Conference of the American College Personnel Association, Boston, MA.

Broughton, E., & Neyer, M. (2001). Advising and counseling student athletes: New Directions for Student Services, *93*, 47–53. https://doi.org/10.1002/ss.4

Cunningham, G. B., & Rivera, C. A. (2001). Structural designs within American intercollegiate athletic departments. *The International Journal of Organizational Analysis*, *9*(4), 369–390.

Davis, B. G. (1987). Beyond ws and ls: Evaluating intercollegiate athletics programs. *New Directions for Institutional Research*, *56*, 37–47. https://doi.org/10.1002/ir.37019875606

Doumas, D. M., Haustveit, T., & Coll, K. M. (2010). Reducing heavy drinking among first year intercollegiate athletes: A randomized controlled trial of web-based normative feedback. *Journal of Applied Sport Psychology*, *22*(3), 247–261. https://doi.org/10.1080/10413201003666454

Dudley, B. S., Johnson, D. W., & Johnson, R. T. (1997). Using cooperative learning to enhance the academic and social experiences of freshman student athletes. *The Journal of Social Psychology; Philadelphia, 137*(4), 449–459. http://dx.doi.org.ezaccess.libraries.psu.edu/10.1080/00224549709595461

Kuh, G. D., Jankowski, N., Ikenberry, S. O., & Kinzie, J. L. (2014). *Knowing What Students Know and Can Do: The Current State of Student Learning Outcomes Assessment in US Colleges and Universities*. Champaign, IL: National Institute for Learning Outcomes Assessment.

Marcello, R. J., Danish, S. J., & Stolberg, A. L. (1989). An evaluation of strategies developed to prevent substance abuse among student-athletes. *The Sport Psychologist, 3*(3), 196–211. https://doi.org/10.1123/tsp.3.3.196

Nite, C. (2012). Challenges for supporting student-athlete development: Perspectives from an NCAA Division II athletic department. *Journal of Issues in Intercollegiate Athletics, 5*(1), 1–14.

Padgett, V. R., & Reid, J. F. (2002). Five year evaluation of the student diversity program: A retrospective quasi-experiment. *Journal of College Student Retention: Research, Theory & Practice, 4*(2), 135–145. https://doi.org/10.2190/25T7-3BBF-6HYB-NHAY

Petitpas, A., Danish, S., McKelvain, R., & Murphy, S. (1992). A career assistance program for elite athletes. *Journal of Counseling & Development, 70*(3), 383–386. https://doi.org/10.1002/j.1556-6676.1992.tb01620.x

Ryska, T. A. (2002). Leadership styles and occupational stress among college athletic directors: The moderating effect of program goals. *The Journal of Psychology, 136*(2), 195–213. doi: 10.1080/00223980209604150

Schroeder, P. J. (2010). A model for assessing organizational culture in intercollegiate athletics. *Journal of Issues in Intercollegiate Athletics, 3*, 98–118.

Schuh, J. H. (2009). *Assessment Methods for Student Affairs*. San Francisco, CA: Jossey-Bass.

Slack, T., & Parent, M. M. (2006). *Understanding Sport Organizations: The Application of Organization Theory*. Champaign, IL: Human Kinetics.

Southall, R. M. (2001). Good start, the bad, and much better: Three NCAA intercollegiate athletic department policy responses to criminal behavior by college athletes. *Journal of Legal Aspects of Sport, 11*(3), 269–284.

Stinson, J. L., & Howard, D. R. (2007). Athletic success and private giving to athletic and academic programs at NCAA institutions. *Journal of Sport Management, 21*(2), 235–264. https://doi.org/10.1123/jsm.21.2.235

Suskie, L. A. (2004). *Assessing Student Learning: A Common Sense Guide*. Bolton, MA: Anker Pub. Co.

Thombs, D. L., & Hamilton, M. J. (2002). Effects of a social norm feedback campaign on the drinking norms and behavior of Division I student-athletes. *Journal of Drug Education, 32*(3), 227–244. https://doi.org/10.2190/2UYU-6X9M-RJ65-3YYH

Chapter Seven

Cross-Program Collaboration and Strategic Partnerships
Evolving Models of Strategic Partnership and Inter-Program Collaboration in Athletics

For many students, college can be an overwhelming experience, often frightening, and full of challenges and change (Thieke, 1994). While all college students must study for college-level exams, create new social networks, and often live away from home (Kidwell, 2005), student-athletes' experiences are distinct, with numerous additional challenges (Jolly, 2008; Petitpas & Others, 1995; Wittmer, Bostic, Phillips, & Waters, 1981). Challenges experienced by student-athletes include: (a) the need to balance roles as student and athlete (Adler & Adler, 1987), (b) feelings of isolation from the student body and faculty (Broughton, 2001; Chartrand & Lent, 1987; Danish, Petitpas, Hale, 1993), (c) time management challenges (Danish et al., 1993), and (d) pressure in assuming leadership roles in the highly commercialized college sport environment (Lapchick, 2006). While researchers have increasingly recognized that intercollegiate student-athletes have additional and specific needs in the process of transitioning both to and from college, they also recognize that understanding the struggles and needs of student-athletes is insufficient to providing them the support and resources often needed for success. In other words, while understanding is imperative, institutions and their athletic departments need to establish innovative programs to target student-athletes' needs beyond support and services provided to the general student population. Such programming, however, presents challenges beyond the capacity of a single program or entity to provide. It is, therefore, that student affairs practitioners working within intercollegiate athletics work to develop strategic partnerships, within and without the university, to marshal resources and leverage the appropriate expertise necessary to deliver effective transitional programming.

In response to this pressing and increasing need for resources, athletic departments across NCAA Division I, II, and III have begun to explore innovative partnership models to support the growing field of transitional programs in intercollegiate athletics. From their genesis in programs focused on life after sport, broader programming designed to support myriad aspects of student-athlete personal and professional development over the last decade, and programs offering opportunities for student-athletes to explore career paths outside the realm of athletics and sport, institutional approaches have now expanded immensely in breadth and scope. The costs associated with these expansions have ballooned as well, in both pecuniary terms and in the human costs related to securing manpower and the necessary expertise. Today, the need for athletic-specific fundraising and development has created a need for new roles and dedicated professionals who not only understand the needs of student-athletes and models of programming to support them, but also who can engage in partnerships across campus, in the community, and globally—and who can effectively work together to weave a strong and seamless fabric of programming around student-athletes.

Currently, student-athlete practitioners are charged with overseeing and delivering multiple and broad areas of programming that serve different aspects of student-athletes' needs. While these areas are distinct enough to warrant or require specialization, today's student-athlete practitioner must at the very least have an awareness and basic knowledge of several key content areas, including personal enhancement, community engagement, leadership development, career development, SAAC, and alumni engagement. Moreover, as these areas of programming are often delivered by separate units, today's practitioners must develop a newer critical skill that can be leveraged to bring these components together, namely the ability to identify and pursue strategic partnerships.

This chapter focuses on the importance of those strong and strategic partnerships in creating high-impact, expert, well-resourced, and sustainable programming to support student-athletes. To illustrate the growing centrality of collaboration and partnerships, this chapter focuses on a model developed by Rutgers University in its efforts to develop a comprehensive model of student-athlete support that brings together high-impact programming incorporating these diverse areas. Rooted in, and informed by, contemporary research on student-athletes' transitions and development in college, Rutgers' Office of Leadership Development and Strategic Partnerships endeavors to deliver quality supportive experiences for Scarlet Knights now and in the future. Figure 7.1 shows Rutgers' Leadership Academy Curriculum Model and Figure 7.2 the Programmatic Pillars.

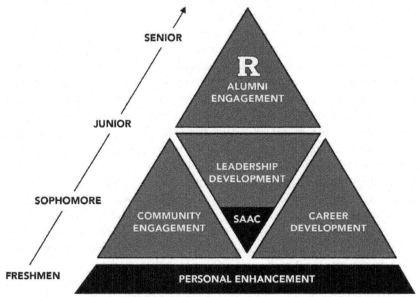

Figure 7.1 Rutgers' Leadership Academy Curriculum Model

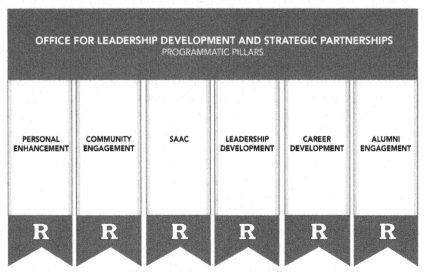

Figure 7.2 Programmatic Pillars

PERSONAL ENHANCEMENT

Rutgers' athletic department is committed to following best practices in student-athlete programming and strives to innovate its offerings based on the most recent literature and findings in the field. The first opportunity for Rutgers' athletics support programming to begin having an impact on student-athletes is in the first year of school. In its model of student-athlete development, the first year is given primacy, in part due to its obvious chronological position in student-athletes' academic careers, but also because the literature is unequivocal about the importance of the first year to all students in general and student-athletes in particular. Specifically, this is accomplished via a credit-based course focused on identity development of the student-athletes. This is a crucial component to the Rutgers Leadership Academy as individuals transition to college and develop an understanding of what it means to be a student-athlete.

According to Reason, Terenzini, and Domingo (2006), because of the cognitive development that takes place during a student's first year of college, students' experiences as freshmen have an oversized importance in their success. Further, Keup (2007) notes that, based on portrayals in media and popular culture, first-year students often enter college with a false sense of confidence and unrealistic expectations. As a result, they often make the mistake of assuming that college will not differ substantially from more familiar high school experiences (Kidwell, 2005). As students' initial first-semester assignment deadlines approach, however, their sense of confidence fades, replaced by an emerging realization that "coasting" through college is not an option. This initial shock can often result in students being "scared straight, as they realize they must take responsibility for their education" (Kidwell, 2005). Research has also consistently shown that during the first-year experience, many students progress through a multidimensional adjustment processes as they (a) make cognitive adjustments in response to navigating and responding to the rigors of college work, (b) undertake a process of emotional development as they discover new concepts of self and a new sense of identity, and (c) engage in dimensions of psychosocial development as they make new friends and establish peer groups (Keup, 2007; Kidwell, 2005; Reason, Terenzini, & Domingo, 2006). Due to the critical nature of the changes students undergo during this period of adjustment, universities have increasingly needed to provide additional support to their students through intentional, well-designed, and high-impact first-year experience programming that lays the groundwork not only for future academic success, but also career success. Moreover, research has also suggested that students arriving at college today are doing so with a greater need of support that is above and beyond what has previously been provided in a systematic, intentional manner.

The first-year experience's importance in laying the groundwork for students' ensuing collegiate experience is due, in part, because it is then that they must first learn to take ownership of their academic performance and begin to build relationships with mentors (Brown, 1981). It is perhaps unsurprising that for many years a student's initial academic performance, measured by first-year GPA, has been considered one of the single most important university attrition indicators (Brown, 1981). Reason et al. (2006) concur that the first year of college is the foundation on which subsequent academic success develops. Donahue's (2004) work has described ways the first-year experience serves as a foundation for academic performance, and has demonstrated that college students' emotional connection, regard for, and attachment to their institutions of higher education are each positively correlated with academic performance. To meet students' desires for intellectual and personal support, Donahue (2004) supports creating positive out-of-the-classroom learning environments that encourage community building and help students develop interpersonal connections with mentors.

Informed by the work of these scholars, and others, the Rutgers Athletics Office of Leadership Development and Strategic Partnerships (LDSP) has pursued a data-driven approach in its firm commitment to the holistic development and personal enhancement of all student-athletes, coaches, and staff. Given its outsized influence in student-athlete success, personal enhancement programs begin in the freshman year as LDSP resources are marshaled toward giving student-athletes an intentional and supportive environment as they develop a sense of personal identity. This focus on authentic leadership and personal identity builds throughout their undergraduate experience as student-athletes continually broaden their focus to include outreach as well as wellness and inclusion programs.

The range of programming and resources leveraged by the Office of LDSP reframes the freshman year into an environment of personal enhancement, laying the foundation for first-year students as they learn to understand and navigate the complex identities they will take on as part of the contemporary student-athlete experience. Programs in the freshman year focus on identity development to equip students with tools and strategies to enhance their personal college success.

LEADERSHIP DEVELOPMENT

A second pillar of the Rutgers model of student-athlete development focuses on providing student-athletes with ample opportunities to cultivate leadership skills that can serve them on the field, court, in classes, careers, or in life. The focus on developing leadership skills is derived from an emergent theme across the literature describing the student-athlete experience. Specifically, the theme concerns how student-athletes must develop critical leadership skills to not only succeed as athletes and students, but also in life after sport (Lapchick, 2006). Such leadership skills are made all the more necessary given today's media-driven environment, in which college athletes are often treated as role models who are likewise expected to assume leadership positions—on and off the field—by virtue of their participation in elite sport competition (Lapchick, 2006). The need for leadership development training as part of the student-athlete experience, as a result, is a necessary component of a holistic support approach and requires research-based transitional programming for student-athletes.

Research by Eiche, Sedlacek, and Adams-Gaston (1997) that examined the attitudes and behaviors associated with success during competition and in life after competition ends shows that specialized leadership training for student-athletes is essential during their time in school. Wittmer, Bostic, Phillips, and Waters (1981) have also shown that, beginning as early as 1991, the increased commercialization and the hyper-competitive nature of college sport could be seen intensifying the transition for student-athletes moving into career fields, in addition to leadership demands related to their sports. Pope and Miller (1999) and Umbach, Palmer, Kuh, and Hannah (2006) contend that student-athletes, particularly in the big-time revenue-producing sports of football and men's basketball, tend to identify as athletes first and students second.

Overall, this body of literature reinforces that student-athletes' needs with respect to transitional programming are distinctive compared to those of the regular student body, specifically when considering the pressures of today's media and commercialized competition environment. Taken together with the fact that transitional programming for first-year student-athletes often provides the necessary foundation for career decision-making and maturation processes which occur during later in a student-athletes' schooling (Danish et al., 1993), it is critical that institutions develop programs that incorporate leadership development and training, and that those programs begin in the initial stages of a student-athlete's academic career. As Lapchick (2006) concludes, additional leadership programming is essential to prepare student-athletes for the challenges of balancing their roles as students and athletes while navigating life events during what amounts to a significant period of transition. However, while such transitional programming must be intentionally designed to consider student-athletes' distinctive needs, it should not be delivered to student-athletes in isolation, segregated from other campus-wide initiatives provided to all students (Umbach et al., 2006).

Drawing on the practices recommended by this literature and other similar studies, Rutgers' Athletics Office of LDSP has employed data to drive its commitment to the continual leadership development of all student-athletes, coaches, and staff. Specifically, the LDSP has developed and implemented an innovative program called the Rutgers Leadership Academy (RLA), which is a formal credit-based partnership with the Rutgers University Graduate School of Education. The RLA intentionally focuses on helping students develop an understanding of leadership theory to help shape and inform their personal actions. Student-athletes are invited to apply leadership theories they learn in class to real-world situations in an athletics context, and to explore how they can be used to better lead and influence peers. They draw upon case studies to inform leadership actions pertaining to emotional and cultural intelligence. By partnering with the Graduate School of Education, the RLA is able to provide a high-impact curricular experience for student-athletes that also carries course credit. In addition to helping student-athletes understand their own personal identities, develop as future professionals, and become leaders in athletics and in life, the for-credit aspect contributes to participants' academic transcripts and progress as students, as well as provides additional incentives for them to take the curriculum and its rigors seriously. This pillar is of significant importance as it helps student-athletes to develop an understanding of personal leadership and then transfer these leadership skillsets to their athletic, academic, and life-after-sport pursuits.

CAREER DEVELOPMENT

Rutgers' approach to supporting student-athlete development begins, in the second year, by incorporating explicit career development programming. Again, while providing student-athletes with support in their exploration of career fields and opportunities has become commonplace across higher education, Rutgers' approach is rooted in, and informed by, the most applicable research available.

While career development theorists differ in terms of the specifics in how they describe the development process, as well as the specific approaches they prescribe to best support it, overall findings are consistent in suggesting that the higher education experience is a dynamic, staged psychosocial process rather than a static, linear phase of life (Hall & Nougaim, 1968; Osborn, Howard, & Leierer (2007); Super, 1957). The body of research addressing student-athletes' distinct needs prescribes career development programming designed to prepare student-athletes for career fields after competition ends that are informed by a process view, rather than an isolated program or experience (Baldwin & Blackburn, 1981). Since students can greatly benefit from additional support throughout the higher education experience, career development must be approached as an evolutionary process and consider that different student groups have different needs (Baldwin & Blackburn, 1981).

Researchers argue that career development courses can be an effective means to help student-athletes transition to career fields after their intercollegiate experience. Collins (1998) reports in a study conducted by the National Association of College and Employers that more than half of the four-year institutions surveyed in the study supported the career development process through formal courses, and the proportion of schools to implement such programming continues to increase. In assessing the impact of various models of programming designed to promote career decision-making efficacy, Reese and Miller (2006) studied a group of 30 undergraduate students enrolled in an introductory career development course. The findings of their research suggest that student-athletes who took the course had a greater level of perceived career decisiveness, specifically with respect to setting career goals and creating a career trajectory plan.

Similarly, research conducted by Davis and Horne (1986) suggests that career courses enhance the educational experience and transition from higher education. As noted, Collins' (1998) study with the National Association of College and Employers revealed that the number of institutions providing such courses is growing. Clearly, institutions have recognized the need for career development programming, prompting faculty and administrators to continue to provide programming opportunities for students, as well as strengthen programs that are already in place.

To inform the process of developing new programs and reframing those already in operation, research has illustrated the importance of rooting career development programming from the perspective of an evolutionary process rather than a static event. This fundamental orientation to the field is supported by the fact that a majority of literature focused on career development describes development as an evolutionary process. This orientation is captured in work by Holland, (1997) who draws a clear connection between one's personality and environment. His theoretical framework, regarded as one of the most influential in the field of career counseling, is manifested in a career assessment tool that enables students to understand interests and obtain career clarity through categorization of strengths and weaknesses, likes and dislikes. Gottfredson (2003) notes that while Holland's assessment tool is commonly used in industrial and organizational behavior disciplines, this assessment tool can be beneficial to students during the higher education experience as it enables them to reflect on their strengths and weaknesses and understand how their skillset fits certain majors and career fields.

Additional research discusses career development as an evolutionary process and notes the importance of developing self-efficacy or confidence in career decision-making during the higher education experience. Betz and Luzzo (1996) studied 627 undergraduate students and measured six variables of confidence. Findings suggest confidence in career decision-making can be mediated significantly by students' confidence with respect to academic skills acquired during the higher educational process (Betz & Luzzo, 1996; Taylor & Betz, 1983). Therefore, helping students to engage in the process of developing and acquiring a "career development skillset" from the foundational first year of the higher education experience is paramount to beginning what the research describes as a multi-stage career decision-making process. While the themes commonly found throughout the career development literature often discuss the student body at large, many of the findings, implications, and prescriptions are applicable to student-athletes as well. Still, a significant gap remains in the amount of direct research into how career development programming can best serve populations with distinctive challenges and characteristics such as student-athletes.

Despite relative immaturity in the field with respect to student-athlete-specific studies on career development, the larger body of research on career development practices in higher education provides a well-supported set of approaches to inform programming. Informed by this body of research, Rutgers Athletics has infused its approach to career development for student-athletes with principles and best practices that have been tested and verified in practice. Beyond a commitment to the constant career development of student-athletes during campus and in life after sport, programming ensures that student-athletes will have ample opportunities to develop an understanding of career and professional development strategies that can shape their personal career trajectories and exploration of potential majors and fields of study. To this end, the Office of LDSP works to support student-athletes as they transition to life after sport by providing intentional, directed assistance by giving students opportunities to complete developmental and behavioral assessments to inform their self-reflection. These assessment instruments provide student-athletes with information about themselves that they would not otherwise have been likely to obtain, and then LDSP staff assist them in understanding and interpreting their assessment results. These structured conversations provide needed support as student-athletes learn how to successfully develop a professional network and employer relations strategy. This pillar is significant because student-athletes tend to focus on the process of career development at the conclusion of their playing careers. The intentional focus of career development throughout the four-year progression is intended to prepare student-athletes for life after sport.

SAAC

As noted elsewhere in this book, the development and participation of SAAC in student-athlete support programming is an important aspect of how programming is administered, but also provides student-athletes with an exceptional opportunity to practice their developing skills in a real and meaningful context. Administration of these dynamic and impactful programs benefits from the perspectives of those they seek to serve. While rooted, in part, in the value of shared governance, utilization of SAACs to help oversee programs is also supported by research showing how these organizations not only enhance the quality, relevance, and impact of those programs, but that participation in them also weaves together sets of experiences that address student-athletes' distinctive developmental needs.

Researchers who study student-athlete career development have returned again and again to a common set of themes with respect to student-athletes' distinctive needs and how to address them. Above all else, however, those studying student-athletes agree that intercollegiate athletes are a distinctive population with characteristics and needs—as well as programmatic needs—that differentiate them from the larger student population in at least three ways (Carodine, Almond, & Gratto, 2001; Danish et al., 1993; Lally & Kerr, 2005). Implications and recommendations of their research suggest that the developmental programming institutions offer and deliver to student-athletes must be designed to address those differences directly.

First, since career development programming must be multifaceted to address the multifaceted career development process, it must also be flexible enough to be highly individualized to the needs of what is a highly diverse population. When designing and administering such programs, practitioners must consider those differing needs if they expect to provide meaningful programming and opportunities.

Second, many studies in the body of literature focused specifically on student-athlete career development programming highlight the importance of identity and the need to assist student-athletes as they (often) struggle to associate and identify with roles other than that of "athlete" (Einarson & Matier, 2002; Finch, 2007; Murdock, 2010). These studies describe the diversity in approaches institutions have taken to create environments and experiences that support that important identity development.

Third, given the multifaceted programming approaches many athletic departments currently use to deliver high-impact experiences and support, researchers suggest that traditional assessment methods for these programs and contexts, including the development of clear assessment tools, can be difficult (Sandstedt et al., 2004).

With these three distinctive programmatic needs in mind, Rutgers Athletics mobilizes its programmatic efforts to support student-athletes by leveraging the SAAC and experience-informed expertise and perspectives of its members. The committee provides guidance and feedback when changes or new facets of programming are being considered. By definition, SAAC is the governance structure for Rutgers' Varsity athletics program. As a leadership body, it represents 24 Varsity sport programs as well as the cheer, dance, and mascot spirit squad. The primary charge and role of the Scarlet Knights SAAC is to:

- Provide a voice for student-athletes to the administration
- Serve as a leadership body on campus and in the community
- Promote an inclusive environment for all student-athletes.

The SAAC sits at the hub of the Office of LDSP, where it is well positioned to assist administrators in developing and shaping programming for student-athletes. Members of the group, for example, regularly provide their feedback by serving as a pilot group for programs. They also provide leadership across the department and among their fellow student-athletes. This group of individuals is instrumental in communicating ideas and policies to the 700 plus student-athletes, and members of the committee serve as liaisons between the university's administration and student-athlete body. While the group is involved in a full range of programs, policies, and practices that impact the student-athlete experience, they focus, in particular, on educational opportunities related to career enhancement and exploration, as well as community engagement and leadership development opportunities. This is a crucial component to the department as it serves as the pilot body for all curricula and the voice of the student-athletes to the administration.

COMMUNITY ENGAGEMENT

Another pillar in Rutgers' approach to, and model for, student-athlete support programming is the high value put on community engagement. Community engagement provides rich opportunities for student-athletes to interact with a diverse range of people outside of athletics, outside of academics, and out in the "real world." Still, aside from providing institutions and athletic departments with a nearly bottomless well of positive press opportunities and ways to ensure a strong relationship between sports, the community, and the fans, student-athletes' participation in a broad range of activities and events categorized under the rubric of "community engagement" is also well supported in the literature exploring student-athlete development.

Fostering opportunities for students to increase their engagement with different kinds of communities is another important component of a productive first-year experience that, in addition to having been an increasing focus of first-year programs across higher education, is also a high-impact practice that is supported in the literature (Reason et al., 2006). Numerous researchers have suggested that encouraging first-year students to develop communities—both in and out of the classroom—helps them to encounter diverse ideas. In practice, this diversification assists students develop relationships with mentors in the school community (Jordan & Denson, 1990; Reason et al., 2006), and these mentors help support students' personal, academic, and professional development. Unsurprisingly, perhaps, students who fail to develop these types of mentorship and community connections are at a higher risk for needing campus mental health services and dropping out before reaching graduation (Arkoff et al., 2006). Ultimately, first-year students tend to thrive when they feel a sense of community and connection with the university, when their learning experiences focus on providing opportunities for mentoring and community engagement, and when their learning environments help them to foster a greater sense of ownership over the direction of their education and academic success (Arkoff et al., 2006; Jordan & Denson, 1990; Reason et al., 2006). These research findings outline a number of specific high-impact program practices that student affairs professionals can adopt to better prepare students for success during their transition into college. Moreover, the findings can also be used to inform approaches to supporting student-athletes, a specialized group within the larger student body, during critical transition periods.

Informed by such findings, and following its data-driven approach, the Office of LDSP is committed to providing student-athletes with opportunities to develop relationships with individuals and organizations in the community. Specifically, the Knights Give Back program focuses on providing student athletes opportunities to develop their confidence, poise, and leadership qualities by giving back to the community, interacting with the general public in a range of events and experiences that both community members and the student-athletes share in the program's commitment to servant leadership. To provide a range of such opportunities, the LDSP office works diligently to cultivate strong, mutually beneficial relationships with community, campus, and global partners. This intentional focus on developing strong partnerships with external organizations and entities allows the LDSP to support a range of opportunities for student-athletes to engage with others outside of the academic and sport environments. Through their participation, the student-athletes not only develop their own character and skills, but they provide the community with talented, engaging leaders who are often respected by the community due to their affiliation with the university and their relationship to athletics and competitive sport. While the program's name, Knights Give Back, implies that the student-athletes are offering their capacities and services to the larger community, the reality is that the carefully cultivated relationships the program has developed provide student-athletes as much value as is gained by the community. The service opportunities, campus collaborations, and international experiences offered by the program provide a rich set of experiences—focused on enhancing cultural intelligence and interpersonal communication—that offer student-athletes high-impact environments in which to develop characteristics and skills aligned with what the literature has shown student-athletes need most to be successful in college and beyond. This pillar is significant as it specifically enables the athletic department to demonstrate value to the community and campus via numerous intentional partnerships. It also helps to foster an understanding of servant leadership.

ALUMNI ENGAGEMENT

Increasingly, the athletic department and the professionals and administrators working to support student-athletes—including at Rutgers—have looked for ways to engage and leverage alumni to enhance student-athletes' experiences, as well as opportunities to develop throughout their college years. Such practices, while often a winning proposition due to the multifarious benefits of keeping alumni engaged with the institution and athletic programs, are also rooted in research about the kinds of experiences that are most beneficial to student-athletes during their struggles to form positive identities and explore various career pathways.

Brown, Glastetter-Fender, and Shelton (2000), for example, have explored the relationship between student-athlete identity and career decision development. Similar to Meyer's (2003) study, Brown et al. (2000) focused on the construct of self-efficacy. Moreover, they examined the additional construct of identity foreclosure, defined as a student-athlete's ability to identify with a role other than athlete. In their study of 189 collegiate student-athletes, participants completed a survey on sport participation and their expectations of turning professional in their given sport. Results show that few students recognize they will become professionals in their sport and highlight once again how student-athletes—all too often—lack exposure to viable alternative career paths (Brown et al., 2000).

Overall, findings from studies that have focused on career development for student-athletes argue that they are a distinctive group in how they struggle to envision themselves in career roles, specifically careers external to athletics. Therefore, greater exposure to other career fields is needed (Baillie & Danish, 1992; Pearson & Petitpas, 1990; Brown et al., 2000).

Themes in the literature highlight, specifically, the need for intentional transitional programming designed to help student-athletes mature with respect to career decision-making and career readiness, and many researchers note that transitioning beyond higher education to a specific career field is a multifaceted process (Brown et al., 2000; Harrison & Lawrence, 2003; Irons, 1999; Taylor & Betz, 1983). Therefore, in addition to addressing specific concerns and needs of the student-athlete population, programming must address them, appropriately, within each step of the development process. Student-athletes themselves note that small rather than large group-session programming better meets their needs for establishing relationships with mentors and for identifying with career roles outside that of athlete (Blann, 1985; Harris, Altekruse & Engels, 2003; Jolly, 2008; Watt & Moore, 2001). Such research supports approaches in which practitioners assist student-athletes not only by navigating the transition out of higher education, but also by establishing meaningful relationships during their time as a student-athlete (Watt & Moore, 2001).

Current practitioners can employ these research findings to inform their programming and to ensure it enables student-athletes to build strong and meaningful mentoring relationships throughout the various stages of their higher education experience. Program directors can facilitate this process by requiring student-athletes to participate in mentorship programs outside the athletics department (Jolly, 2008; Watt & Moore, 2001), because while mentorship programs internal to athletics can provide relationships outside of one's sport, they often do not provide such relationships outside the larger "athletic" tent. The best programs, however, very intentionally provide student athletes with opportunities to develop relationships with mentors in current professional roles outside athletics (Jolly, 2008). By pairing student-athletes with mentors in the community or campus at large, student-athletes can be exposed to career fields outside the confines of intercollegiate athletics (Watt & Moore, 2001), providing them with a richer array of career pathways and models to draw upon while developing a plan for life after sport. Overall, the literature suggests that institutions cultivate programming that includes real and timely opportunities for student-athletes to develop meaningful mentorship relationships outside athletics to enable a more successfully transitional model as they move from higher education to career fields.

Informed by the data, suggested practices, and findings outlined in the literature, the Rutgers Athletics Office of LDSP aims to support members of the Scarlet Knight family during their intercollegiate experience and in life after sport by offering student-athletes opportunities to be mentored outside of the context of athletics. Specifically, the LDSP cultivates such opportunities via continual alumni engagement, most recently by bringing the Varsity R Letterwinners Association into the Office of LDSP. As the LDSP works to engage current student-athletes and former student-athletes, the Varsity R Letterwinners Association and LDSP share a common goal of enhancing professional networks and mentorship opportunities across many generations of Scarlet Knights.

STRATEGIC PARTNERSHIPS

In addition to creating and administering programs that intentionally support each of the six pillars, student-athlete development professionals are charged specifically to collaborate across both internal and external entities within the athletic department and campus as a whole. In essence, student-athlete development professionals must have a keen awareness of both the internal and external operations of an intercollegiate athletic department. This hybrid role places those filling these positions into an increasingly important space for both internal and external partnership development. Figures 7.3–7.6 show the Credit-Based, Rising Knights Freshman, Emerging Leaders Sophomore, and Veteran Leaders Junior curricula respectively.

Internal Partnerships. First, to be most successful the cumulatively programmatic partnerships that develop from the above curricula are nested in a comprehensive model of wraparound support services for the student-athletes. Figure 7.7 displays an example holistic Student-Athlete Excellence Leadership Team.

In this case study specific strategic partners within academic support, compliance, LDSP, sports health, sports nutrition, sports performance, sport psychology and Title IX/units conduct work together in a model that has become known on campus as the Student-Athlete Excellence Team. Each of these areas specifically touches the student-athlete directly and therefore influences the student-athlete experience on a daily basis. These individual units gather once monthly to discuss issues facing student-athletes and identify solutions that can be developed across departments.

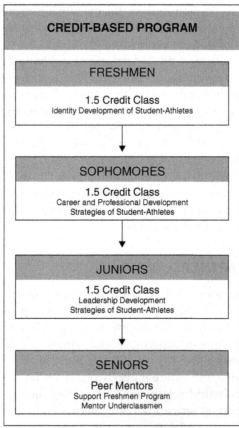

Figure 7.3 Credit-Based Curriculum Model

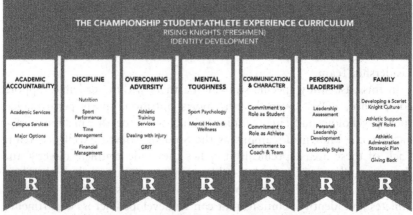

Figure 7.4 Rising Knights Freshman Curriculum

Figure 7.5 Emerging Leaders Sophomore Curriculum

Figure 7.6 Veteran Leaders Junior Curriculum

Student-athlete development professionals, while not experts in every one of the aforementioned areas, must serve as strong communicators and advocates to bring all parties to the table so that student-athletes and the programs that support them can benefit from the expertise of professionals from each area. While working together to develop and enhance programming to support their students, student-athlete development professionals can serve a vital role in fostering cross-campus and cross-community communication so that all members of the student-athlete support team can operate effectively and efficiently.

EXTERNAL PARTNERSHIPS

In additional to internal communication, collaboration, and partnerships, student-athlete development professionals are being increasingly thrust outward, beyond the university and into the space of external relationships. As such, contemporary student-athlete development professionals must cultivate a general awareness of the nuances of corporate sponsorship and philanthropic giving as athletic departments utilize this area of goodwill in conversations on a range of topics including: providing mentorship and internship opportunities for student-athletes, sponsorships, and generating

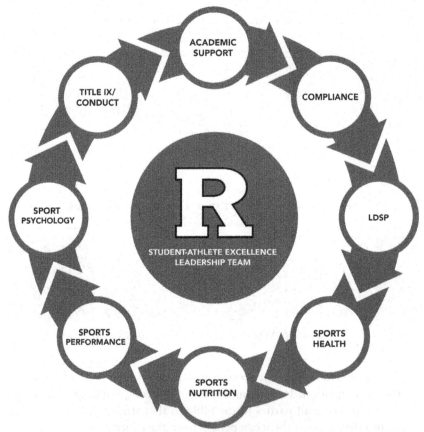

Figure 7.7 Holistic Student-Athlete Excellence Leadership Team

revenue in ways that make support programs more robust and sustainable. Figure 7.8 is a model of external strategic partnerships.

Corporate Sponsorship. Today, corporate entities operate with a keen awareness of the value student-athletes can bring to their workforces. Many companies value the work ethic, sense of purpose, motivation, and drive that student-athletes have learned over the course of their college experience. In fact, the last decade has seen an enhanced focus on how student-athlete development professionals interface with the world of corporate sponsorship. Schools looking to start programs and expand programs are increasingly turning to corporate giving opportunities as they seek new revenue outlets. For example, institutions that exist in close proximity to large metropolitan areas may begin my developing a needs assessment of inventory points and programs for sponsorship. In a second stage, they may then identify corporations and organizations that share common

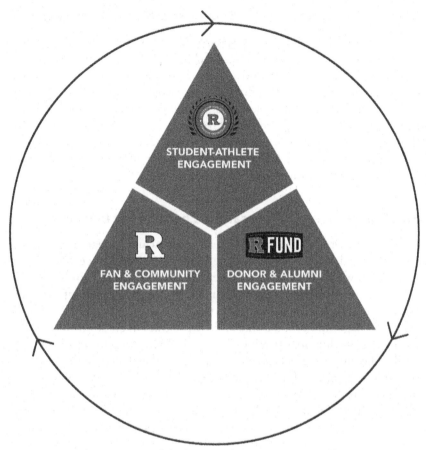

Figure 7.8 Model of External Strategic Partnerships

needs or values to diversify the workforce with hungry, motivated, and disciplined individuals. By demonstrating solutions to corporate problems, student-athlete development professionals can become intimately involved with success at corporate sponsorship fulfillment efforts.

Developing a Corporate Sponsorship Platform. As corporate entities continue, and increasingly express interest in leveraging the excitement, history, personalities, and brand identification of athletic programs by hiring student-athletes, developing points of engagement—or inventory points for sponsorship—is an increasingly popular way for athletic departments and institutions to support their programs financially. The steps outlined below are a basic model that student-athlete development professionals might take to develop mutually beneficial strategic relationships with corporate entities.

Step 1: Identify a Corporate Sponsorship Manager on Campus

At the Division I level, corporate sponsorship is typically administered by a third-party entity (such as IMG or Learfield) that will manage the rights to an extensive range of assets that are of interest to potential corporate sponsors. For example, these entities may manage diverse mediums such as signage, radio, TV, and print as well as other developing mediums for corporate branding and exposure. Understanding who should be involved in conversations, as well as the range of desirable media, is the first key step, and campus representatives will need to work with these companies to gather the appropriate professionals from campus and beyond to gather around the table.

Step 2: Developing a Proposal and Engaging the Company

Once the proper individuals have been identified and brought together, the next step of identifying points of engagement can commence. Specifically, individuals will work together to identify areas that speak to the mission of corporate entities that wish to hire student-athletes or support specific community engagement efforts but that are also in keeping with the mission, image, and brand of the athletic program in question. When identifying partnership opportunities, it is critical that campus representatives work diligently to select corporate sponsors that enhance the brand of the athletic program, build capacity and identity, and—importantly—are unlikely to bring negative connotations, press, or disfavor to the program.

For example, an athletic department might entertain engaging corporate partners within the context of the career development pillar of a program in ways that would provide opportunities for corporate HR managers to interact directly with student-athletes in mock interview or career settings. In such a partnership, however, the company in question would necessarily be one of high esteem and reputation, not just any company seeking partnership.

Step 3: Fulfillment

Once a tentative, mutually beneficial sponsorship agreement has been reached, it is important for campus representatives to outline the parameters of the agreement so areas of expectation are fully understood by both sides and can be fulfilled. The corporate partners will need to provide detailed documentation to both the institution and its corporate headquarters documenting the parameters of its participation, including the scope, deliverables, responsibilities, and shared goals. Depending upon the extent of these partnerships, as well as the range of funding and sponsorship involved, these agreements may require collaboration with the institution's office of general council, include liability and other insurance considerations, and may need to follow delineated contracting regulations—especially in public institutions, where rules may be dictated by government regulations or other rules.

Philanthropic Giving. In addition to funding partnerships, many corporate donors have interest in supporting programs for the purpose of providing an opportunity to give back across a wide breadth of programs and student-athletes. Today's institutional fundraising and development units are becoming more and more entwined with the office of student-athlete development. For example, at Rutgers University, the Senior Associate Athletics Director for LDSP is charged with "R Fund" fundraising responsibilities as the RLA seeks to become a privately funded entity. In turn, student-athlete development programs can be helpful in conversations with large donors who have interest in the student-athlete experience.

Process of Cultivating Support. The process of developing a sustainable funding mechanism is highly dependent upon the ability of the student-athlete development staff to collaborate intentionally with the fundraising or development officer. The process a student-athlete development leader might follow to begin collaboration with the development and fundraising arm of the athletic department is presented below.

Develop the Departmental Relationship

In many NCAA departments, the individual responsible for developing and maintaining fundraising relationships is referred to as the Director of Development. When student-athlete development professionals who have minimal background in fundraising are presented with promising fundraising or partnership opportunities, they would be best advised to seek out the support of their university's trained, dedicated development officers, in particular those internal to the athletic department. This is often the best first stop for identifying areas of intersection and partnership, as well as the potential for larger-scale "asks" down the road. This level of collaboration is crucial to identifying strategic partnerships as well as for creating processes for cultivating donors who are passionate about student-athlete development and fundraising.

Develop Collateral or Program Overview

In the world of development (fundraising), "collateral" is a term used to describe a "leave-behind packet" that donors can refer to as they seek to understand if their giving interests align with the mission and values of specific programs. Developing a high-level booklet that overviews the

COLLABORATION AND STRATEGIC PARTNERSHIPS

Figure 7.9a LDSP Overview Booklet

program's interests, developmental opportunities, and points of alignment can be foundational to making the ask (see Figure 7.9a and b).

Identify Engagement Points

As development officers meet with potential donors, they will often present a menu of items that are strategic programmatic priorities to the

Figure 7.9b LDSP Overview Booklet

department, but are presented as interest areas or program opportunities for the athletics department or unit they are representing. It is critical, therefore, for the department to have specific student-athlete development programs and other programmatic experiences, activities, or opportunities appear within this menu of items, and that the list presented to a particular potential donor/partner be relevant to their interests. As a student-athlete development leader, professionals can identify what their signature areas of engagement will be with respect to the different programmatic areas of oversight. For example, Rutgers University specifically organizes curricula around six pillars. As a result, engagement points can be offered to potential donors related to each of these six pillars. Each donor will have different areas of interest, and therefore a wide variety of intentional and meaningful engagement points are critical.

Alumni Engagement. Finally, many student-athlete development units are now coming in closer contact with the letterwinner associations at their respective institutions. Letterwinner organizations that comprise former Varsity student-athletes create an immediate tie to professional networks, which in turn can be leveraged in a range of other support activities and programming—many discussed throughout this chapter. These individuals tend to have an enhanced affinity to give back via their time, talent, and treasures. Properly utilizing and engaging alumni can lead to sustained success of student-athlete development programs specifically pertaining to mentorship and career development.

As Rutgers Athletics Office for LDSP continues to expand its programming and external influence, it has become a priority to seek opportunities to independently fund and monetize the office. Historically, the majority of funds raised by LDSP have been private donations made by a relatively small group of individuals and their companies. Though these donors have been a fantastic source of wealth, wisdom, and work over the past decade, the costs associated with providing comprehensive, high-impact student-athlete support programming has made it a necessity for LDSP to pursue strategic corporate sponsorships, philanthropic giving, and alumni engagement sources of revenue. Figure 7.10 shows a value-added fundraising proposal.

1) Do your homework.
    Oftentimes, student-athlete development professionals will not be the ones making the ask. However, they will be the individuals in the room selling the program and describing the value programs bring to the lives of student-athletes. When meeting with major donors, understanding their personal needs and values is crucial. In turn, completing background research in partnerships with your development office can assist with conversations and pitches.

2) Continue to engage.
    Many times, major gifts take months or years to solicit. The process of stewarding donors is a delicate balance. Some will want to have a clear idea of what they are investing in while others who are more entrepreneurial in mindset will view a student-athlete development

THE VALUE
Intentionally impact 700 student-athletes on an annual basis

BE A PART OF THE GROWTH MINDSET
The Rutgers Leadership Academy, SAAC and other programs internal to LDSP aim to collectively support a personal growth culture for all members of the Rutgers Athletics Department and Scarlet Knight family.

MULTIFACETED PROGRAM INVOLVEMENT OPPORTUNITIES

Alumni and Career Development Event Involvement

- Knight of Networking Invitation - Our largest signature event involving 200 student-athletes across diverse majors in a roundtable networking environment
- Site visits to employment sites supported by LDSP-opportunity for groups to tour and visit with members of your organization one-on-one or in a small group
- R Awards Student-Athlete Success Invitation

Personal and Leadership Development for Student-Athletes

- Opportunity to speak to student-athletes within the context of the Rutgers Leadership Academy credit based program
- Affiliation with key levels of the Academy (i.e., SAAC, Rising Knights, Emerging Leaders, Veteran Knights programs)

Community Service and Corporate Social Responsibility Support

- Opportunity to engage and/or associate with 700 student-athletes annually who serve over 100 organizations in the Greater New Brunswick Campus and New Jersey Community in the Knights Give Back Program
- Provide foundational support for student-athletes' professional, personal, and leadership development through philanthropic involvement

22

Figure 7.10 Value-Added Fundraising Proposal

program or unit like that of a startup business. While the latter is less intense on behalf of the development officers in terms of engaging a donor, targeted follow-up is crucial. Enabling a donor to specifically see, feel, and touch the program in its early stages can enhance buy-in.

3) Fulfillment.
Whether you are involved in large major gift asks or smaller philanthropic giving opportunities with major donors, fulfilling promises is important. In turn, constant communication with the development office and external/marketing arms of the department is crucial to ensure individuals are seeing and feeling the value of their gifts.

155

REFERENCES

Arkoff, A., Meredith, G. M., Bailey, E., Cheang, M., Dubanoski, R. A., Griffin, P. B., & Niyekawa, A. M. (2006). Life review during the college freshman year. *College Student Journal, 40*(2), 263-269.

Baillie, P. H. F., & Danish, S. J. (1992). Understanding the career transition of athletes. *The Sport Psychologist, 6,* 77-98.

Baldwin, R. G., & Blackburn, R. T. (1981). The academic career as a developmental process: Implications for higher education. *Journal of Higher Education, 52*(6), 598-614.

Betz, N. E., & Luzzo, D. A. (1996). Career assessment and the career decision-making self-efficacy scale. *Journal of Career Assessment, 4*(4), 413-428. https://doi.org/10.1177/106907279600400405

Blann, F. W. (1985). Intercollegiate athletic competition and students' educational and career plans. *Journal of College Student Personnel, 26*(2), 115-118.

Broughton, E., & Neyer, M. (2001). Advising and counseling student athletes: New Directions for Student Services, *93,* 47-53.

Brown, C., Glastetter-Fender, C, & Shelton, M. (2000). Psychosocial identity and career control in college student-athletes. *Journal of Vocational Behavior, 56,* 53-62.

Brown, P. (1981). Programs for first-year students. *Forum for Liberal Education, 4*(1), 2-16.

Carodine, K., Almond, K. F., & Gratto, K. K. (2001). College student-athlete success both in and out of the classroom: New Directions for Student Services, *93,* 19-33.

Chartrand, J. M., & Lent, R. W. (1987). Sports counseling: Enhancing the development of the student-athlete. *Journal of Counseling and Development, 66*(4), 164-167.

Collins, M. (1998). Snapshot of the profession. *Journal of Career Planning & Employment, 41*(2), 32-36.

Danish, S. J., Petitpas, A. J., & Hale, B. D. (1993). Life development intervention for athletes: Life skills through sports. *Counseling Psychologist, 21*(3), 352-385.

Davis, R. C., & Horne, A. M. (1986). The effect of small-group counseling and a career course on career decidedness and maturity. *Vocational Guidance Quarterly, 34,* 255-262.

Donahue, L. (2004). Connections and reflections: Creating a positive learning environment for first-year students. *Journal of the First-Year Experience & Students in Transition, 16*(1), 77-100.

Eiche, K., Sedlacek, W. E., & Adams-Gaston, J. (1997). *An exploration of leadership characteristics in college athletes* (Research Report No. 6–97). Retrieved December 1, 2009 from ERIC database.

Einarson, M. K., & Matier, M. W. (2002, June). *More alike than not? An examination of what differentiates intercollegiate athletes from their classmates.* Paper presented at the Annual Forum for the Association for Institutional Research Toronto, Canada.

Finch, B. L. (2007). Investigating college athletes' role identities and career development (Unpublished doctoral dissertation). Texas A & M University, College Station, Texas.

Gottfredson, L. S. (2003). The challenge and promise of cognitive career assessment. *Journal of Career Assessment, 11,* 115–135.

Hall, D. T., & Nougaim, K. (1968). An examination of Maslow's need hierarchy in an organizational setting. *Organizational Behavior and Human Performance, 3,* 12–35.

Harris, H. L., Altekruse, M. K., & Engels, D. W. (2003). Helping freshman student athletes adjust to college life using psychoeducational groups. *Journal for Specialists in Group Work, 28*(1), 64–81.

Holland, J. L. (1997). *Making Vocational Choices: A Theory of Vocational Personalities and Work Environments.* Odessa, FL: Psychological Assessment Resources.

Irons, J. (1999). Life after sports: The career transition of African American male student athletes (Unpublished Master's thesis), University of Michigan, Ann Arbor, Michigan.

Jolly, J. C. (2008). Raising the question #9: Is the student-athlete population unique and why should we care? *Communication Education, 57*(1), 145–151.

Jordan, J. M., & Denson, E. L. (1990). Student services for athletes: A model for enhancing the student-athlete experience. *Journal of Counseling and Development, 69*(1), 95–97.

Keup, J. R. (2007). Great expectations and the ultimate reality check: Voices of students during the transition from high school to college. *NASPA Journal, 44*(1), 3–31.

Kidwell, K. S. (2005). Understanding the college first-year experience. *Clearing House: A Journal of Educational Strategies, Issues and Ideas, 78*(6), 253.

Lally, P. S., & Kerr, G. A. (2005). The career planning, athletic identity and student role of identity of intercollegiate student-athletes. *Research Quarterly for Exercise and Sport, 76*(3), 275–285.

Lapchick, R. E. (2006). *New Game Plan for College Sport.* Westport: Praeger Publishers.

Meyer, K. J. (2003). Influences on career decisions of college student-athletes (Unpublished honors thesis). Northwestern University, Evanston, IL.

Murdock, C. M. (2010). Identification of best practices of the CHAMPS/Life Skills program: perspectives of Division I college and university athletic department administrators (Unpublished doctoral dissertation). Lamar University, Beaumont, Texas.

Osborn, D. S., Howard, D. K, & Leierer, S. J. (2007). The effect of a career development course on the dysfunctional career thoughts of racially and ethnically diverse college freshmen. *The Career Development Quarterly*, 55, 365–376.

Pearson, R. E., & Petitpas, A. (1990). Transition of athletes: Developmental and preventive perspective. *Journal of Counseling Development*, 69, 7–10.

Petitpas, A. J., & Others, A. (1995). Counseling athletes: A new specialty in counselor education. *Counselor Education and Supervision*, 34(3), 212–19.

Pope, M. L., & Miller, M. T. (1999). *Support services for student-athletes: Athletic department and student affairs officers' perceptions* (Research Report No. 143). Retrieved December 1, 2009 from ERIC database.

Reason, R. D., Terenzini, P. T., & Domingo, R. J. (2006). First things first: Developing academic competence in the first year of college. *Research in Higher Education*, 47(2), 149–175.

Reese, R. J., & Miller, C. D. (2006). Effects of a university career development course on career decision-making self-efficacy. *Journal of Career Assessment*, 12(2), 252–266.

Sandstedt, S. D., Cox, R. H., Martens, M. P., Ward, D. G., Webber, S. N., & Ivey, S. (2004). Development of the student-athlete career situation inventory (SACSI). *Journal of Career Development*, 31(2), 79–93.

Super, D. E. (1957). *The Psychology of Career: An Introduction to Vocation Development*. New York: Harper and Rowe.

Taylor, K. M., & Betz, N. E. (1983). Applications of self-efficacy theory to the understanding and treatment of career indecision. *Journal of Vocational Behavior*, 22(1), 63–81.

Thieke, W. S. (1994, November). *Developmental change in freshman students: Validating Chickering's theory of student development*. Paper presented at the Annual Meeting of the Association for the Study of Higher Education, Tucson, AZ.

Umbach, P. D., Palmer, M. M., Kuh, G. D., & Hannah, S. J. (2006). Intercollegiate athletes and effective educational practices: Winning combination or losing effort? *Research in Higher Education*, 47(6), 709–733.

Watt, S. K., & Moore, J. L., (2001). Who are student athletes? New Directions for Student Services, *93*, 7–18.

Wittmer, J., Bostic, D., Phillips, T. D., & Waters, W. (1981). The personal, academic, and career problems of college student athletes: Some possible answers. *Personnel and Guidance Journal, 60*(1), 52–55.

Chapter Eight

The Future of Student-Athlete Development

Throughout this book, we have endeavored to present an overview of contemporary practice in intercollegiate athletics, broadly construed, and in so doing, provide practitioners with a valuable resource to guide their practice in supporting student-athletes. We hope that by reading this book, or specific chapters within, that those working, or aspiring to work in the field of student-athlete support or program administration will come away with valuable background information on intercollegiate athletics, including: descriptions of the historical and contemporary contexts of athletics, synthesis, and discussion of research exploring the impacts of mixing athletic competition and the pursuit of education, challenges to successful outcomes for student-athletes, as well as frameworks of cognitive, affective, psychosocial, and leadership development programs.

Likewise, we have included discussion of models of programming designed to support various aspects of the student-athlete experience, contextualized case studies of comprehensive and holistic programming provided by institutions at the Division I, II, and III levels, guidelines to conducting assessment and evaluation of practices in intercollegiate athletics support programming, strategic partnership and fundraising approaches, and identification of trends that can be observed across these diverse topic areas. In other words, we hope that the information and discussion in this book will help to enrich the practice of those working with student-athletes or help to prepare those seeking to begin a career working with them.

As we worked to assemble the materials in this book and engaged one another in conversation about what to include or leave out, mention in passing, or highlight, one observation or overarching theme kept coming up again and again: the field of practice surrounding the support of intercollegiate athletes is dynamic and is undergoing constant and significant change. Moreover, the pace of change within the field has accelerated rapidly in the last two decades.

The approaches that institutions have employed to support student-athletes have evolved over time, from the first offerings in the 1970s and mandated programming in the early 1990s, to today's comprehensive support services. What might originally have been an advisor working with both general students as well as athletes, has now begun to include impressive student-athlete academic facilities, large staffs, and specialized learning resources. The introduction of new academic metrics by sport governing bodies has created new needs, including helping former college athletes complete their degrees and ensure all athletes find meaningful career options. Moreover, the spotlight in recent years on concussions in college and professional sports has pushed institutions to focus not just on "return to play" protocols but also on "return to learn" policies. Overall, there has been a growing recognition that student-athletes need, and deserve, multifaceted programming that supports their distinctive needs in school, on the field, and beyond.

Model programs at the University of Nebraska, WCU, and UW-Whitewater demonstrate the focus on the holistic development of student-athletes, regardless of the resources available. Programs that engage strategic partners across fundraising and corporate areas of the athletics department are now becoming increasingly prevalent. Gone are the days of support programs that operate in isolation from the rest of the athletics department and academic institution. Institutions and higher education leaders now realize they must make a significant investment in their student-athletes, especially considering that these students dedicate a significant amount of time to sport-related activities as well as represent their colleges and universities in communities and as a public face. In return, and at the very minimum, additional resources and staff with a focus on their education and life after sport is a reasonable exchange.

STUDENT-ATHLETE DEVELOPMENT PROGRAMS OF THE FUTURE

The area of student-athlete development has also seen continued growth over the past 20 years. As scholars have increased their focus on the student-athlete population, and their research has demonstrated a need for personal developmental support, organizations such as the NCAA and N4A have intentionally focused on how to best prepare professionals who work with student-athletes during their collegiate experience. The historical evolution of programming is in direct response to the intense focus on the student-athlete experience, their time demands, and the need to prepare student-athletes for life after sport as professionals in career fields. Student-athletes now experience better support than ever before, yet organizational change continues. Professionals working with student-athletes at the collegiate level now have access to multiple avenues for support and professional development.

In athletic department leadership positions, more administrators rising through the ranks are coming from student-athlete services units than ever before, even in AD roles. As a result of student-athlete services administrators' overseeing many areas beyond academics (e.g., mental health and well-being, nutrition, diversity and inclusion), advancing professionals in the field have more experience and knowledge in their toolkit within athletic department internal operations. Leaders in student-athlete support services also are involved in sport oversight and supervise more than just full-time employees, since many departments hire their own tutorial staff that can be quite sizeable. The expertise from student-athlete affairs leaders continues to be recognized as valuable for athletic senior staff roles. It does not hurt that colleges and universities, at their very core, have academic missions, so athletic departments should align their mission with those of their institutions. Having expertise in academics and student-athlete development is necessary for athletic department leadership, and recently, professionals in those areas have advanced to these areas more than ever before. In the future, student-athlete development will continue to be a focus and in the conversation at the leadership table. Athletic department senior leaders will have a solid understanding of what these units do and how they serve student-athletes for success both on and off of the field or court.

STANDARDIZING THE PROFESSION OF STUDENT-ATHLETE DEVELOPMENT

Recognizing the need to standardize the profession, the N4A developed a call to action to enhance the training and development of student-athlete development professionals. Specifically, in the summer of 2018, the first-ever PDI for student-athlete development professionals brought together a formal faculty to create a standardized curriculum housed within the N4A organization. While the Steve McDonnell PDI program has existed for 15 years, this marked the first instance of programming specifically targeted for student-athlete development professionals. The inaugural PDI's mission was to create and maintain a learning community that transmits, creates, and preserves the knowledge that defines the profession. After completion of the program, PDI graduates receive continuous professional development and are connected to the other members of their class. All PDI tracks come together at the annual conference to celebrate new graduates and network with each other. Since the first PDI track was offered in 2005, graduates are linked together through various ways digitally and then through intentional conference activities annually. These established connections provide a space for the sharing of best practices and innovative programming ideas too.

N4A PDI Program History. PDI was created with the vision to provide an innovative professional development experience for individuals seeking to excel in the field of student-athlete support services. Initiated by the leadership of N4A Past-President Steve McDonnell, PDI began as a pre-convention event at the N4A 30th anniversary convention and was hosted by North Carolina State University in 2005. The inaugural institute focused on leadership and management and it was designed for individuals who have been in the field five to ten years and have demonstrated leadership potential. The institute has expanded and now currently consists of five tracks: Leader/Manager, New Practitioner, Learning Specialist, HBCU, and Student-Athlete Development (N4A, 2018).

Student-Athlete Development PDI Program Overview. College athletics is constantly changing. There are always new considerations and new roadblocks that impact how we shape culture and the student-athlete experience. This evolution and fluctuation are made even more challenging by what seems to be a constant lack of funding and resources to improve the student-athlete experience. Because of this, it is essential that as professionals, we learn to identify new sources of revenue and innovative solutions through our current positions in student-athlete development. Throughout the PDI, participants have an opportunity to look deeply at the challenges and issues they are facing in their athletic departments. They then design a solution and "pitch" to receive funding for their program(s). The PDI institute is taught by faculty in the field that marry the concepts of scholarship and practitioner work in higher education.

Program Objectives. Drawing from the contemporary needs of practitioners who work with student-athletes and the landscape of higher education and athletics, the PDI program is designed to provide a deeper understanding of the current landscape and challenges in college athletics and how it impacts their work and departments. In addition, the curriculum seeks to educate industry leaders and practitioners on practical ways to communicate, lead, and develop themselves, their teams, and their departments. As units and departments continue to grow the PDI institute aims to provide a collaborative workspace for professionals to build upon their skillsets, network, and learn from others while allowing professionals the opportunity to develop specific solutions for adapting and programming to the constantly evolving landscape of college athletics. The faculty meet regularly throughout the year to plan curricula and ensure materials are both current and relevant to professionals in the field.

Student-Athlete PDI Program Components. To achieve these objectives, the program integrates the following components:

1. Leadership Development
2. Personal Development
3. Career Development
4. Social Responsibility
5. Community Engagement
6. Diversity and Inclusion
7. Strategic Planning

In the next decade, program development, assessment scholarship, and practitioners through organizations like N4A will continue to provide additional data to guide the field and help those working in student-athlete development to best support college athletes. The PDI specifically for student-athlete development professionals will continue to be offered on a biannual basis with the intent of enhancing the development of individuals who aspire to leadership roles in student-athlete development. This industry standard attempts to qualify and quantify measures of a strong student-athlete development program, regardless of resource level or the student-athlete population size.

LESSONS LEARNED: HISTORICAL EVOLUTION OF STUDENT-ATHLETE SUPPORT PROGRAMS

While student-athlete academic support services have been in place since the late 1980s across NCAA athletic departments, their primary focus has been to maintain eligibility (Murdock, Strear, Jenkins-Guarnieri, & Henderson, 2016). By 1991 the NCAA issued a specific call to action to increase specialized programming at the campus level to focus on the holistic development of student-athletes. Through collaborative efforts of the NCAA and the NCAA member institutions, the NCAA CHAMPS/Life Skills program was created, which centered on five pillars including academic excellence, athletic excellence, personal development, career development, and community service (Murdock et al., 2016). Consistent with the challenge to develop quality student-athlete development programs, the NCAA required all member institutions to implement some version of this five-pillar curriculum. However, at the campus level, program implementation has varied widely, and student affairs professionals often lacked curricular guidance (Navarro, 2012). Campus implementation differed not only because utilizing the pillars to inform programming was the singular requirement for institutions to follow, but also because the NCAA life skills implementation requirement existed solely at Division I member institutions. Regardless, to the benefit of the student-athletes on their campuses, many Division II and III institutions have adopted aspects of life skills programs, and some have gone as far as to implement entire curricula.

In 2014, the NCAA initiated a call to action across each division to enhance programming for the quickly emerging area of student-athlete development. In turn, a call went out to develop action teams to work toward a national curriculum to prepare student-athletes for life after sport. These action teams were intended to provide additional campus-level "train the trainer" support for campus-based life skills professionals. Shortly thereafter, the NCAA Division of Leadership Development announced a partnership with the National Association of Academic Advisors for Athletics (now N4A: National Association of Academic and Student-Athlete Development Professionals), a merger intended to further support professionals who desired to prepare student-athletes for life after sport. Over a three-year period, the N4A worked with the NCAA to merge programming. In turn, the rebranded N4A organization has become the primary provider of development and programming for life skills professionals (NCAA, 2019). This rebranding marks a crucial time in collegiate sport as substantive professional development exists for those working to support student-athletes for the first time. As the organization matures, and more and more professionals engage with one another, the potential to move the field forward through sharing of resources and best practices can only benefit the quality of the support offered to tomorrow's student-athletes.

RECOMMENDATIONS FOR ADMINISTRATORS: SUPPORTING COLLEGIATE ATHLETES FOR LIFE AFTER INTERCOLLEGIATE SPORT

Examining and synthesizing empirical research studies focused on the student-athlete higher education experience is crucial for developing high-impact programs that best serve this unique population. This is of particular importance as new emphases emerge, such as approaches for preparing athletes for life after college. The literature supports the need for specialized transitional programming for the student-athlete subset, but has recognized that complete segregation from the study body can be detrimental. Therefore, contemporary athletic administrators must strike a careful balance between specific student-athlete programming and programming that encourages campus-wide interaction and engagement.

Though it is not always feasible, athletic departments might seek partnerships with their institutions' career centers to dedicate a percentage of a career professional's time to working with student-athletes. Alternatively, they might hire a career development professional to work solely with athletes. Whether in their courses, in advising, or targeted support programming, student-athletes must learn the importance of articulating their transferable skills from athletic participation to the workplace, which will serve them well during the interview process.

Administrators should also seek opportunities to encourage student-athletes for leadership roles at the institutional, conference, and national levels of sport governing bodies. The NCAA offers leadership conferences and careers in sports forums for student-athletes. Many campuses offer leadership academy programs, boards like SAAC, and other leadership development programs through mentoring or other means. Team captains are not the only leaders among student-athletes, so there should be further investment in development of student-athletes beyond athletic-related leadership roles.

In addition, individuals should consider developing programs that specifically speak to the programmatic standards developed by the N4A, including leadership development, personal development, career development, social responsibility, community engagement, diversity and inclusion, and strategic planning. Now more than ever, athletic departments are expanding their staff in student-athlete support services to include more student-athlete development specialists. As APR-based revenue distribution begins in 2020, meaning the NCAA will distribute revenue based on student-athletes' surpassing academic metrics, there will be more funding to invest in student-athlete development. Administrators should conduct site visits with peer institutions in their conference and division to get an idea of best practices and innovative programming at institutions with different resource levels. Job descriptions in this field are constantly evolving and changing, and administrators will play a big role in shaping the future of this field.

IMPLICATIONS FOR THE EVOLUTION OF NCAA POLICY AND GOVERNANCE ON THE STUDENT-ATHLETE EXPERIENCE

Budgetary constraints and priorities experienced by institutions and athletic departments across NCAA divisions share some similarities, but also key differences that impact how leadership and personal development is fostered in student-athletes. Constant, however, is the shared believe in the concept of the "student-athlete." During the Division I Men's Basketball Tournament every year, the NCAA runs a commercial that inspiringly packages and delivers the NCAA's mission and vision across divisions, which emphasizes the goal of a balance between student and athlete. Last year's debut of a new commercial (replacing the original) closed with "if you have the drive to succeed in school and sports, we'll provide the opportunity" (NCAA, 2019). Symbolically, this statement signals a commitment to student/athlete identity harmony. Berkowitz and Schnaars (2017) have noted this commitment across Division I by highlighting that since the 2011–2012 academic year, athletics-related financial aid has increased every year, including an almost 9% spike last year. This funding increase is consistent with Berkowitz and Schnaars' (2017) assertion that students succeed at higher rates when provided financial aid and other support services (such as specific support staff and programming). Still, Berkowitz and Schnaars (2017) indicated that many of the increases found their way into "administrative staff compensation," a category that masks the type of staff as well as whether or not increased funding also provided resources for student-athletes. Clear priorities and transparent accountability structures might better bring about campus-based culture shifts that include increasing spending for specific student-athlete programming consistent with DiMaggio and Powell (1983).

Since the establishment of the NCAA life skills pillars, many changes and modifications have been made to how institutions support student-athletes. In addition, programming and policy are beginning to evolve as student-athlete development professionals now have a professional training hub recognized by the NACDA, the umbrella organization that oversees N4A's operations. Like any program initiative, quality of campus-level programs can be enhanced through clear objectives, sound research, and input of stakeholders. Student-athlete development professionals must commit to working together to hone a guiding curriculum, maintain clear assessment measures, and ensure program continuity at the campus level with national standards as outlined in the N4A PDI shared earlier in this chapter.

Research supports a seeming programmatic dilemma for student affairs practitioners who work with student-athletes. Namely, these individuals must work to offer programming strictly for student-athletes that serves unique needs while also attempting to provide inclusive opportunities for student-athletes to participate in campus-wide career development events. This balance can be exhausting and lead to high levels of burnout for current practitioners (Rubin & Moreno-Pardo, 2018). Student-athlete services professionals must consider their own self-care before serving students (Rubin & Moreno-Pardo, 2018). Now that an infrastructure is in place, campus administrators must continue to advocate for resources that benefit student-athletes across divisions. The case studies presented in Chapter 5 demonstrate that it is possible to have robust programming within all three NCAA divisions, regardless of institution or athletic department size, or resource levels.

IMPLICATIONS FOR CAMPUS STUDENT-ATHLETE DEVELOPMENT PRACTITIONERS

Current practitioners can use emerging research findings, guidance provided by N4A, and data-driven NCAA recommendations to guide campus-level programming. By considering a model that includes a four-year approach, practitioners can prioritize initiatives year by year. In essence, program continuity can be increased if practitioners are not seeking to accomplish five different pillars in a single year. Instead, each year could focus specifically on certain components of the suggested pyramid, each building upon the former. Practitioners should root program design, assessment, and evaluation in empirically based learning outcomes related to student-athlete development. Building and delivering a structured curriculum such as this will only serve to reinforce principles of research for quality time on task and purposeful involvement (Renn & Reason, 2012).

In order for student-athletes to be able to integrate curricular content and experiences into their sense of self and their burgeoning leadership identity, practitioners need to provide several ongoing opportunities for guided and self-guided reflection. This reflection needs to focus on student-athletes' experiences in the campus environment, in terms of both this physical environment, and the environment student-athletes feel. Renn and Reason (2012) noted that this will aid in crystallization of learning. While each campus is different, student affairs professionals who work with student-athletes can enhance programming if given proper guidance. The NCAA framework that provides a common understanding of holistic development may better assist campus-level student affairs practitioners who struggle not only to justify new programming, but balance athletics and academic worlds. Ideally, the transition of responsibility from the NCAA to N4A in this area will provide practitioners with the skills and resources necessary to follow through on this work (Leach, 2015).

Establishing programming and curricular development as a priority sends signals internally to the department and externally to the institution, and by emphasizing departmental mission, staff performance evaluations, reward structures, and professional development, those who supervise student-athlete support staff can communicate that serving all student-athletes individually is important (Tierney, 1988). This type of symbolic and cultural shift can also signal to student-athletes, as well as others who interface with an athletic department (e.g., tutors, faculty, other support staff), that the environment is one in which key decision-makers value student-athlete development (Renn & Reason, 2013). For the students they work with, staff in other departments whom they partner with, and other staff within the athletic department, practitioners should make an effort to communicate that "best practice" implementation actually enhances work that is already underway (DiMaggio & Powell, 1983). This stylistic approach is important, because culture change requires buy-in from all parties involved.

RECOMMENDATIONS FOR PRACTITIONERS

Practitioners might consider the following suggestions as they develop comprehensive programs:

Personal Enhancement. Programs in this area must be committed to the holistic development of all student-athletes, coaches, and staff. For student-athletes, personal enhancement programs should begin in the freshman year as the unit intentionally focuses on supporting student-athletes as they develop a sense of personal identity. This focus on authentic leadership and personal identity should build throughout their undergraduate experience as student-athletes focus on outreach, wellness, and inclusion programs. Programming in the freshman year lays the foundation as student-athletes learn to understand the complex identities of the contemporary student-athlete experience. Programs in the freshman year should focus on identity development to equip students with tools and strategies to enhance their personal college success.

Leadership Development. Leadership development programs should be committed to the continual leadership development of all student-athletes, coaches, and staff. Many institutions may wish to adopt a leadership academy or seek to develop a formal credit-based partnership with an Academic Department that intentionally focuses on developing an understanding of leadership theory to shape personal action. Student-athletes should apply leadership theory to real-world situations in an athletics context to lead and influence peers. A formal leadership curriculum for student-athletes can support them as they seek to understand their own personal identity, develop as future professionals, and become leaders in athletics and in life. Student-athletes may draw on case studies to inform leadership action pertaining to emotional and cultural intelligence.

Career Development. Career development programs should be committed to the ongoing career development of student-athletes during campus and in life after sport. Student-athletes should develop an understanding of career and professional development strategies to shape their personal career trajectory and major exploration. Quality programs should work to support student-athletes as they transition to life after intercollegiate sport. To this end, practitioners should intentionally help students complete developmental and behavioral assessments, such as the Strong Interest Inventory, to inform intentional self-reflection. Programs should support student-athletes as they learn how to successfully develop a professional network and employer relations strategy.

Engaging SAAC. The SAAC is the governance structure for all NCAA athletics program. The primary function of SAAC is to:

- Provide a voice for student-athletes to the administration
- Serve as a leadership body on campus and in the community
- Promote an inclusive environment for all student-athletes.

Within quality programs, the SAAC serves as a pilot for programs and leadership voice across the department. This group of student-athlete team representatives is instrumental as a communication hub for student-athletes and serves as a liaison between the administration and student-athlete body. Student-athlete support services professionals should all be familiar with the student-athletes on SAAC, not just the group's staff advisor. That way, SAAC is familiar with all of the staff as well as the depth and breadth of programs and services offered by the support unit. This is also a way for these student-athlete leaders to tell their teammates more about the programs and services.

SAAC members should be able to provide input in programming stages. One or two members can rotate through staff meetings so a student voice is present when the support unit meets, especially if it is not a unit that meets regularly. Some support units comprise one person or a two-person team, so more input from student-athlete leaders would be beneficial anyway and might develop some volunteers if there are areas of interest by the students. SAAC members also can connect support units with different student-athletes on their teams based on their academic and career interests. If student-athletes are helping with career programming, they can share suggested fields or alumni from their teams in different work environments to the professionals planning the event.

Community Engagement. Quality engagement programs should focus on developing a program culture that is committed to giving back to the community. Community engagement programs should focus on providing shared experiences to foster servant leadership. Student-athlete development professionals can seek to intentionally support opportunities to engage with the community, local schools, campus, and global partners. Through service opportunities, campus collaborations, and international experiences, practitioners can provide a strong focus on enhancing cultural intelligence and interpersonal communication.

Strategic Partnerships and Alumni Engagement. While strategic partnerships and alumni engagement is relatively new in the area of student-athlete development, it is crucial to a comprehensive program. Student-athlete development professionals should seek to support student-athletes not only during their intercollegiate experience, but also in life after sport via continued alumni engagement. Practitioners may consider making letterwinner associations internal to the department to best engage current student-athletes and former student-athletes. Quality programs can leverage a shared a common goal of letterwinners to enhance professional networks and mentorship opportunities across many generations.

The University of Nebraska offers a networking night annually that brings alumni representing different career fields along with other professionals to engage with student-athletes. Student-athletes are more confident to engage with professionals representing their career interests as the alumni are introduced with pictures and memories from their time as Nebraska student-athletes. The campus career center also provides networking opportunities prior to the event to prepare student-athletes for networking. This is a great way to engage alumni and also connect them with current student-athletes, as they can make a significant impact on their future.

FUTURE STRUCTURAL DEVELOPMENTS

The shift in core competencies and changes in the professional nomenclature lead the field of student-athlete development to widen its net, in essence. Professionals are now overseeing so many aspects of the student-athlete experience, as far-reaching as nutrition, mental health, concussion recovery, and other areas not housed in the athletic academic advising units. Student-athlete development professionals are in a unique position to collaborate with other staff within the athletic department, across campus resources, and in the local community to offer opportunities for student-athletes to have the best holistic development experience during their enrollment. The areas of leadership development, career preparation, personal enhancement, well-being, and financial literacy are just a few of the growing areas of focus within this expanding field. This growth will enhance athletic department leadership as more professionals from student-athlete services units will advance to senior-level positions.

Professionals who truly understand the student-athlete collegiate experience are important contributors to athletic department decision-making and should have a seat at the table. In Chapter 5, the University of Nebraska's life skills leader Keith Zimmer advanced to a senior leadership position on the athletic staff, which he found critically important for the student-athlete population there. Again, the opportunity for athletic department senior staff to include academic and student-athlete development experts can only help athletic departments align with their college or university's academic mission, which ensures consistency and a positive public image.

Student-athlete development professionals can and should work as advocates to bring together the Student-Athlete Support Service units in athletics to enhance collaboration. Such collaboration can be focused on measurable outcomes that enhance internal operations that touch and support the student-athlete. In addition, collaboration between internal units can address issues facing student-athletes, enhance awareness of current trends and issues in the field, and enhance collaboration and troubleshoot processes/challenges for units. Models of collaboration were described in Chapter 5, including Nebraska's AEC group and WCU's cross-campus efforts to eliminate redundancy of support services across campus that benefit student-athletes. As student-athlete time demands require us to develop a comprehensive educational plan for student-athletes, such groups can help to maximize efficiency of time for coaches and student-athletes while improving programs holistically across departments.

According to the NCAA (2019) Race and Gender Demographics Database, athletic academic advisors and life skills coordinators (the titles used to represent the positions discussed in this book) are the most diverse positions within NCAA athletic departments today. The expertise, lived experiences, and passion that come from this unique and diverse group of professionals that support student-athletes bring a rich set of resources and creative ideas to the forefront of this ever-evolving field. Colleges and universities should celebrate this excellence as a model for other units both within athletics and on campus. There is a significant opportunity for student services units across campus to look toward student-athlete affairs professionals and the diverse perspectives and backgrounds they bring to their work.

REFERENCES

Berkowitz, S., & Schnaars, C. (2017, July 6). Colleges are spending more on their athletes because they can. Retrieved from www.usatoday.com/story/sports/college/2017/07/06/colleges-spending-more-their-athletes-because-they-can/449433001/

DiMaggio, P., & Powell, W. (1983). The iron cage revisited: Institutional isomorphism and collective rationality in organizational fields. *American*

Sociological Review, 48(2), 147–160. Retrieved from www.jstor.org/stable/2095101

Leach, K. C. (2015, October 16). *NCAA, N4A to partner on life skills professional development.* Retrieved from www.ncaa.org/about/resources/media-center/news/ncaa-n4a-partner-life-skills-professional-development

Murdock, J. L., Strear, M. M., Jenkins-Guarnieri, M. A., & Henderson, A. C. (2016). Collegiate athletes and career identity. *Sport, Education and Society, 21*(3), 396–410. doi:10.1080/13573322.2014.924920

N4A: National Association of Academic and Student-Athlete Development Professionals. (2018). *PDI history.* Westlake, OH.

Navarro, K. M. (2012). *Toward an understanding of career construction in the 21st century: A phenomenological study of the life experiences of graduating student-athletes at a large highly-selective midwestern university* (Doctoral dissertation) Retrieved from ProQuest (3508437).

NCAA. (2019). *Race and gender demographics database.* Retrieved from www.ncaa.org/about/resources/research/diversity-research

Renn, K. A., & Reason, R. (2012). *College Students in the United States: Characteristics, Experiences, and Outcomes.* San Francisco, CA: Jossey-Bass.

Rubin, L. M., & Moreno-Pardo, M. D. (2018). Burnout among student-athlete services professionals. *Journal of Higher Education Athletics and Innovation, 1*(3), 1–25.

Index

Note: Page numbers in **bold** indicate tables and in *italic* indicate figures.

AASP *see* Accelerated Academic Success Program (AASP)
academic clustering 23, 37–39, 71
Academic Progress Rate (APR) 64, 88, 119, 166
academic support programs 56
academic–athletic role conflict 7, 30, 33–35
ACC *see* Atlantic Coast Conference (ACC)
Accelerated Academic Success Program (AASP) 55–56
activism, student-athlete 18–20
Adler, P. 7, 30, 31, 33, 34, 36, 41, 72, 131
Adler, P. A. 7, 30, 31, 33, 34, 36, 41, 72, 131
African-American student-athletes 12; academic clustering and 38; *see also* Historically Black Colleges and Universities (HBCUs)
After the Game Program 71
Allen, W. R. 8
alumni engagement *133*, 143–145, 154–155, *155*, 171
APR *see* Academic Progress Rate (APR)

assessment 111–129; assessment cycle 117–126, *117*; Boston University case study 126–129, *127*, *128*; challenges 113–114; curriculum maps 8, 119–121, **120**; data analysis 124; data collection 124; defined 7, 112–113; interpretation of results 125; learning objectives 117–119, 121–122; literature 114–116; measure selection 122–124; planning 116–126; purpose 113; rubrics 123–124, **123**
athlete unionization 18–19
Athletes Connected Program, University of Michigan 63–64
athletic departments, role of 22–23
athletic identity salience 33
Atlantic Coast Conference (ACC) 9; *see also* Power 5 conferences
autonomy development 34, 44

Baillie, P. H. F. 8, 40, 41, 144
Banta, T. W. 113
Bell, L. F. 35, 39, 40, 72
Berkowitz, S. 167

174

INDEX

Bernhard, L. M. 72
Betz, N. E. 139, 144
Big 12 Conference 9, 21; *see also* Power 5 conferences
Big Ten Conference 9, 20, 21; *see also* Power 5 conferences
Black, T. 68
Blann, F. W. 33, 144
Blustein, D. L. 33
Boleska, K. 40
Boston University 58, 126–129, *127*, *128*
Brewer, B. W. 7
"bridge" programs 70–71
British Studies programs 68
Broughton, E. 37, 39, 41, 61, 115, 131
Brown, C. 32, 35, 36, 143–144
Brown, Michael 19

career and personal development challenges 32–39; academic clustering 23, 37–39, 71; athletic identity salience 35–36; identity foreclosure 8, 32–33, 35–36, 44, 143–144; isolation from the student body 36–37; Millennial and Generation Z student-athletes 39–42; role conflict 7, 30, 33–35; theoretical frameworks 33–34, 42–46
career construction theory 7, *45*, *46*, 46
career development programs 58, 71, 165–166; assessment 115; recommendations 169–170; Rutgers University case study *133*, 137–140; study abroad 69; Warhawk Leadership Academy case study 98, *99*, 101–102
career identity 7, 32
Career Influences Inventory (CII) 34
Career Maturity Inventory (CMI) 36

Case, B. 37–38
Challenging Athletes' Minds for Personal Success (CHAMPS) 9, 54, 164–165
Chartrand, J. M. 8, 34, 36, 40, 131
Chickering, A. W. 33, 34, 43, 44
Chung, D. J. 24
Clemson University 71
collaborative approaches to student-athlete support 90–93, 95, 97, 109; *see also* Rutgers University case study
Collins, M. 138
Colorado State University 67
Colter, Kain 19
Comeaux, E. 39, 52
community engagement programs 58–59, 101, *133*, 141–143, 170
competence development 34, 43
comprehensive grants 55
comprehensive student-athlete support programs 161; recommendations 169–171; *see also* Rutgers University case study; University of Nebraska case study; Warhawk Leadership Academy case study
concussion management 59–61, *62*, *63*
conference realignment 21–22
Coomes, M. D. 39
Cooper, J. N. 8, 56
corporate sponsorship 148–151
Cote, J. E. 32
Croissant, J. L. 30, 41
cultural intelligence 68
curriculum maps 8, 119–121, **120**

Danish, S. J. 8, 30, 32, 38, 40, 41, 131, 136, 140, 144
Davis, B. G. 113–114
Davis, R. C. 138
Dean, D. R. 39, 40, 41

175

INDEX

DeBard, R. 39
degree-completion programs 64–67, 66
DiMaggio, P. 167, 169
Dimick, K. M. 33, 38
diversity, impacts of athletics programs on 24
diversity programs 67
Division I institutions 13–14, 28; academic clustering 37–39; conference realignment 21; governance 15–16; numbers of student-athletes 23–24; pressure to perform 29–30; scholarship rules 14; support programs 52–53, 55–56; time demands 29; *see also* University of Nebraska case study
Division II institutions 14; conference realignment 21; governance 17; support programs 53, 56; time demands 29; West Chester University case study 90–93
Division III institutions 14–15, 28; governance 17–18; support programs 53; time demands 29; *see also* Warhawk Leadership Academy case study
Donahue, L. 135
Dudley, B. S. 115
Duhon, D. 68
"dumb jock" stereotype 30, 43, 44
Dweck, C. S. 43

Edmonds, Amy 93, 95
Eiche, K. 136
Elmore, T. 40, 41, 42
Emmert, Mark 20
emotion management 34, 44
equivalency scholarships 14
Erikson, E. 33–34

facilities for student-athlete support 72–73, 80–81
faculty athletics representatives (FARs) 16, 23, 79
FBS *see* Football Bowl Subdivision (FBS)
FCS *see* Football Championship Subdivision (FCS)
Federal Graduation Rate (FGR) 119
Finch, B. L. 34–35, 140
Finley, P. S. 37, 38, 41
First-Year Experience courses 71
fixed mindsets 43
Flutie Effect 24
Football Bowl Subdivision (FBS) 8, 14, 16; academic clustering 37–39; pressure to perform 30; time demands 29
Football Championship Subdivision (FCS) 8, 14, 16, 29
Fountain, J. J. 37, 38, 41

Gaston Gayles, J. 40, 42
gender identity 44
Generation Z student-athletes, challenges for 39–42
GOALS study 29
Good, A. J. 33
Gottfredson, L. S. 138–139
grade point average (GPA) 65, 85, 94, 104, 119, 135
Graduation Success Rate (GSR) 64, 82, 88, 119
grants 55–56
Gressard, C. 33, 34, 38
Growth, Opportunities, Aspirations and Learning of Students in College (GOALS) study 29
growth mindsets 43

INDEX

GSR *see* Graduation Success Rate (GSR)

Harris, H. L. 36, 37, 144
Harrison, C. K. 28, 39, 41, 144
HBCUs *see* Historically Black Colleges and Universities (HBCUs)
head count scholarships 14
health and well-being programs 61–64, 115–116; concussion management 59–61, 62, 63
Hicklen, S. 39
Hill, K. 34
Historically Black Colleges and Universities (HBCUs) 8, 12; academic support programs 55–56
Hodes, J. S. 90–93
Holland, J. L. 138–139
homophobia 44
Hope, J. 40, 41, 42
Horne, A. M. 138
Howard-Hamilton, M. F. 34, 37
Hu, S. 40, 42

identity development: role conflict and 33–35; study abroad and 68; theoretical frameworks 33–34, 43–46
identity establishment 34, 44
identity foreclosure 8, 32–33, 35–36, 44, 143–144
inclusion programs 67
initiative grants 55–56
institutions: impacts of athletics programs on 23–24; role of 23
integrity development 34, 46
international travel programs 67–70
interpersonal relationships, developing mature 34, 44
isolation from the student body 36–37

Jewell, J. O. 8
Jolly, J. C. 9, 36–37, 131, 144

Kansas State University 24, 65–67
Kennedy, S. R. 33, 38
Keup, J. R. 134
key indicators 64, 119
Kidwell, K. S. 131, 134
Kramer, D. A. 21

Lapchick, R. E. 29–30, 131, 136
Larsen, V. 67, 68, 69
Lawrence, S. M. 28, 41, 144
Leach, K. C. 2, 9, 54, 168
leadership development programs 40; recommendations 169; Rutgers University case study *133*, 135–137; *see also* Warhawk Leadership Academy case study
learning communities 71
learning objectives 8, 117–119, 121–122
learning specialists 56
Leblanc, Dennis 79, 81, 82, 84, 89
Lent, R. W. 8, 34, 36, 40, 131
letterwinners 9, 171
Levine, A. 39, 40, 41
life after sport *155*; alumni engagement *133*, 143–145, 154–155, *155*, 170–171; defined 9; transition out of college programs 71–72, 136–137, 138, 139, 144–145, 165–166; *see also* career development programs
life skills *see* student-athlete development
Luzzo, D. A. 139

Macalester College 70
McDonnell, Steve 162, 163
McLeod, M. 68
Mamerow, G. P. 71
March Madness 19–20

177

INDEX

Marcia, J. E. 8, 32, 35
media 19–20
mental health support 61–64
metrics 64, 119
Meyer, K. J. 34, 143
Milkman, R. 39
Millennial student-athletes, challenges for 39–42
Miller, C. D. 138
Miller, M. T. 136
mindset theory 43
mission statements 22–23
Moore, J. L. 144
Moreno-Pardo, M. D. 2, 167
Moses, R. A. 30, 36
Murphy, G. M. 32, 33, 35, 36

National Association for Intercollegiate Basketball (NAIB) 12
National Association of Academic and Student-Athlete Development Professionals (N4A) 1–2, 54, 162–164, 165, 166, 167
National Association of College and Employers 138
National Association of Intercollegiate Athletics (NAIA) 12–13, 56–57
National Collegiate Athletic Association (NCAA) 1–2, 12, 13–15; divisional structure 13–15; GOALS study 29; governance 15–18; policy evolution 166–167; scholarship rules 14; support programs 9, 52–54, 55–57, 71, 164–165; TV revenue 19–20; *see also* Division I institutions; Division II institutions; Division III institutions
National Junior College Athletic Association (NJCAA) 13, 56–57

National Labor Relations Board (NLRB) 19
Navarro, K. M. 39, 46, 58, 71, 93, 95, 164
NCAA *see* National Collegiate Athletic Association (NCAA)
networking opportunities 71, 171
Neyer, M. 37, 39, 41, 61, 115
Nichols, Marissa 126–129
NJCAA *see* National Junior College Athletic Association (NJCAA)
NLRB *see* National Labor Relations Board (NLRB)
Northwestern University 18–19

Odenweller, K. G. 39
Ohio State University 72
Oregon State University 22–23, 58

Pacific-12 Conference (PAC-12) 9, 21; *see also* Power 5 conferences
Padgett, V. R. 116
Palomba, C. A. 113
Parker, K. 40
PDI *see* Professional Development Institute (PDI)
personal development challenges *see* career and personal development challenges
personal enhancement programs: recommendations 169; Rutgers University case study *133*, 134–135; Warhawk Leadership Academy case study 98, 99
Petitpas, A. 8, 115, 131, 144
philanthropic giving 151–154, *155*
Phillips, S. D. 33
Pinkerton, R. S. 61, 71, 72
Pizzolato, J. E. 39
Pope, M. L. 136
post-eligibility opportunities (PEO) program, University of Nebraska 84–85, *86*, 87

post-eligibility scholarships 65, 84
Powell, W. 167, 168–169
Power 5 conferences 9, 15, 16, 29
power and influence: student-athlete activism 18–20; traditional sources of 20–21
Professional Development Institute (PDI) 2, 162–164
purpose development 34, 44–46

Race and Gender Demographics Database 172
Reason, R. D. 134, 135, 142, 168
Rebel Reconnect program 65, 66
Reese, R. J. 138
Reid, J. F. 116
Reisser, L. 43, 44
Renick, J. 36, 37, 38, 41
Renn, K. A. 168
retention rates 85, 90, 119
return to learn programs 59–61, 62, 63, 161
Rickes, P. C. 40, 41
role conflict 7, 30, 33–35
Rubin, L. M. 2, 30, 36, 167
rubrics 123–124, **123**
Rutgers University case study 132–155; alumni engagement *133*, 143–145, 154–155, *155*; career development *133*, 137–140; community engagement *133*, 141–143; corporate sponsorship 148–151; curricula *133*, *146*, *147*; leadership development *133*, 135–137; personal enhancement *133*, 134–135; philanthropic giving 151–155, *155*; SAAC *133*, 140–141; strategic partnerships 145–155, *148*, *149*, *152*, *153*, *155*

SAACs *see* student-athlete advisory committees (SAACs)
Savickas, M. L. 7
Schnaars, C. 167
scholarships 14, 56; equivalency 14; head count 14; post-eligibility 65, 84
Schulz, Kirk 20
SEC *see* Southeastern Conference (SEC)
Second Wind program, Kansas State University 65–67
sexual orientation 44
Sharp, L. A. 23
Sheilly, H. K. 23
Sina, J. A. 34, 37
Smith, R. A. 8, 12, 15–16
Snyder, E. E. 35
Southeastern Conference (SEC) 9, 20, 21; *see also* Power 5 conferences
Sowa, C. 33, 34, 38
Spears, J. 40, 42
specialized learning programs 59
stereotypes 23, 30–32, 43, 44
strategic partnerships 131–132, 171; Rutgers University case study 145–155, *148*, *149*, *152*, *153*, *155*
Strong Interest Inventory 170
student-athlete activism 18–20
student-athlete advisory committees (SAACs) 15, 17, 18, 23; recommendations 170; Rutgers University case study *133*, 140–141
student-athlete development 1–2, 54, 57–58; defined 9; future of 161–162; historical evolution of 164–165; practitioner implications 168–169; standardizing profession 162–164
student-athlete experience 28–46; academic clustering 23, 37–39, 71; athletic identity salience 35–36; career and personal development challenges 32–39; identity foreclosure 8, 32–33, 35–36,

44, 143–144; isolation from the student body 36–37; Millennial and Generation Z student-athletes 39–42; myths about 30–32; pressure to perform 29–30; role conflict 7, 30, 33–35; theoretical frameworks 33–34, 42–46; time demands 29, 44
student-athlete support programs 52–73; academic support 54–57; community engagement 58–59, 101, *133*, 141–143, 170; concussion management 59–61, 62, 63; degree completion 64–67, 66; diversity and inclusion 67; facilities for 72–73, 80–81; historical evolution of 164–165; legislation 52–54; mental health and well-being 61–64, 115–116; recommendations 169–171; return to learn 59–61, 62, 63, 161; specialized learning 59; student-athlete development 57–58, 161–162, 164–165, 168–169; study abroad 67–70; targeted tutoring 59; transition out of college programs 71–72, 136–137, 138, 139, 144–145, 165–166; transition to college programs 70–71, 134–135, 142; West Chester University case study 90–93; *see also* assessment; Rutgers University case study; University of Nebraska case study; Warhawk Leadership Academy case study
study abroad programs 67–70
Suggs, W. 38, 41
"summer bridge" programs 70–71
Super, D. E. 7, 137
support programs *see* student-athlete support programs

Suskie, Linda 113
Symonds, M. L. 69

targeted tutoring 59
Taub, D. J. 43–46
Taylor, K. M. 139, 144
time demands 29, 44
training tables 10, 72, 80
transition out of college programs 71–72, 136–137, 138, 139, 144–145, 165–166; *see also* career development programs
transition to adulthood 32
transition to college programs 70–71, 134–135, 142
TV revenue 19–20

Umbach, P. D. 37, 136–137
unionization 18–19
University of Arkansas 57–58
University of California, Berkeley 72
University of Illinois at Chicago 58, 67
University of Michigan 63–64
University of Minnesota 60–61, 62, 63
University of Mississippi 65, 66
University of Missouri 19
University of Nebraska case study 78–90, 171; awards banquet 85–88; culture, brand, and policies 88–90; facilities and budget 80–81; post-eligibility opportunities (PEO) program 84–85, 86, 87; staff 81–82; student-athlete development/life skills programs 82–84
University of Oklahoma 19
University of Richmond 69–70
University of Wisconsin-Whitewater *see* Warhawk Leadership Academy case study

Valentine, J. J. 43–46

Wainwright, P. 68
Warhawk Leadership Academy case study 93–109; administration and staffing 96; campus collaborations 97; career development 98, 99, 101–102; community outreach and engagement 101; identity development 99–101; program evaluation 102–104; program implementation 105–108; program outcomes 104–105; program structure and curriculum 97–102, *98*, *99*
Watt, S. K. 144
well-being programs 61–64, 115–116
West Chester University case study 90–93
Wittmer, J. 131, 136
Wolverton, B. 19, 59, 72
Wright, N. 67, 68, 69

Zimmer, Keith 79–80, 81, 82–84, 85, 89–90, 172

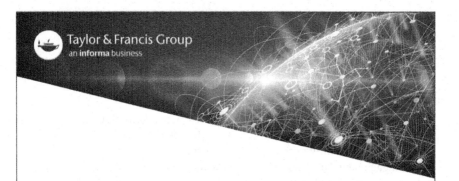